Cinderella's Slipper

225-235-7480

McDougal & Associates
Servants of Christ and stewards of the mysteries of God

Jdyamuto @
Bell South
latt.Net
Highway to Glory

Cinderella's Slipper

If the Shoe Fits ...

by

Jody Amato

Original cover design by Sherie Campbell (sonandshield@comcast.net) is the artist's rendition of Jody's visit to Heaven.

Published by:

McDougal & Associates
P.O. Box 194
Greenwell Springs, LA 70739-0194
www.thepublishedword.com

McDougal & Associates is dedicated to the spreading of the Gospel of Jesus Christ to as many people as possible in the shortest time possible.

ISBN 13: 978-1-934769-00-3
ISBN 10: 1-934769-00-2

Printed in the United States of America
For Worldwide Distribution

Dedication

This book is dedicated:

To my five children: *Michelle, Danny, Tony, Frankie* and *Brandy*, to my *grandchildren* and to my *great-grandchildren.*

To the memory of my parents, *Carthel and Margaret Allen*, and my brother *Duane "Dutch."*

To my sister *Diane*, for her prayers and her love and for believing in me.

To some wonderful people who have helped me in more ways than they could possibly know, *Pat and Warren, Brother and Sister Kenneth Charles* and *John R. Martin.*

To *all of my faithful intercessors.*

Most of all, to *Jesus*, for all He has done for me.

To give unto them beauty for ashes, the oil of joy for mourning, the garment of praise for the spirit of heaviness; that they might be called trees of righteousness, the planting of the LORD, *that he might be glorified.*

Isaiah 61:3

Contents

Foreword by Darlene McCarty

The Bible declares, *"My grace is sufficient for you, for My strength is made perfect in weakness"* (2 Corinthians 12:9, NKJ). Focusing on weakness will only cause a person to live out their life wishing for things that never come. In *Cinderella's Slipper*, Jody Amato walks us through the lives of ladies of both the Old and New Testaments who reached a point where they stopped looking at their weakness and began to concentrate on God's strength. Were these perfect women living a life without problems? I think not!

Each of the women considered in these pages came to a crossroad in her life and had a choice to make. She could allow her past and current circumstance to dictate her future (and she would then live life wearing dirty, ragged, worn-out clothes and walking around in shoes that could only lead her down a road of hopelessness, brokenness, misery and despair). But she had another choice. She could step into Cinderella's tailor-made slippers, slippers that would bring her healing, forgiveness, restoration and regeneration. Can God do that? Well if He can get you from where you were to where you are now, then He can take you from where you are now to where

He wants you to be. And He can do it by perfecting your weakness through His divine strength.

Your past can either delay your destiny or deliver your destiny, and unbiblical responses to circumstances around you always delays it. You may, for instance, throw a pity party, but the only one who will show up for the party is the devil. Biblical responses to your circumstances, on the other hand, will deliver your destiny, and every angelic being will stand cheering you across the finish line. In this powerful book, Jody Amato brings out wonderful biblical principles that will encourage, motivate and propel you into an anointed life, a life designed especially for you on the day of your creation.

Satan knows the power a discerning woman possesses when she walks in God's assignment for her life. The first message sent to him from Heaven was this: *"Out of her [Eve's] seed will come One who will crush your head"* (Genesis 3:15, My paraphrase). That day Satan declared war on woman and her seed. He began his war in the Garden of Eden with Eve, but since that time, his tactics have not changed, and he has not stopped trying to destroy the seed of woman. Today, through Christ, you have the power to break Satan's authority over your home, over your family, over your husband and over your children. And when Satan has lost those battles, he has lost the war!

The assignment God has for you is too great to be sabotaged by your past. Depression and lack of self-worth are illegal for you. Life has done nothing to you that God cannot use for good. He can turn your pain into purpose, your mistakes into a message and your violence into victory. Then you can make a difference in the world around you.

In Jesus' family tree, there are four women mentioned whom I call "the bad girls of the Old Testament." If God can use Rahab (a harlot), Ruth (a former pagan and outcast widow), Bathsheba (an adulteress) and Tamar (the widow who seduced her father-in-law) to bring forth the Son of God, then surely He can use you too.

Most people have a Cinderella story to tell. The people closest to them have mistreated and taken advantage of them, just like Cinderella's mean stepmother and two wicked stepsisters. Like Cinderella, they endure hard labor, dreaming of a prince to come, so that they can enjoy a few good times in life before stepping back into reality when the clock strikes midnight.

In that moment, they realize that nothing has changed. Life hasn't been fair to them. Bad choices have brought bad consequences, and the carriage to take them into their divine destiny has seemingly turned into a pumpkin. The prince and that glass slipper now only seem to be a figment of their imagination. Thus they spend their life dreaming, hoping and wishing for a glass slipper that never seems to come.

There is hope. In these pages, Jody Amato brings out biblical truths (through personal experiences and the lives of women of the Bible) that will obliterate your past, transform your present and launch you into a new season. As you read through this book, healing will begin to take place in your mind, soul and spirit. By making a decision to read the stories transcribed on these pages, you have made a choice to not remain the same person you are today, but to allow God to speak into your life, changing and molding you into His image. I can guarantee you by the time you finish this book, you will not be the same person you were when you began. A new person will emerge.

Watch out devil, women are about to step into their Cinderella's Slipper and walk in places they've only dreamed of, do things they've only talked about and conquer any mountain that gets in their path.

The apostle Paul wrote: *"One thing I do, forgetting those things which are behind and reaching forward to those things which are ahead ..."* (Philippians 3:13, NKJ). The choice is yours. Do you wear shoes of yesterday, accepting life for what it is, for what it could have been or for what you wish it had been? Or will you allow God to place the glass slipper of destiny upon your foot, raising you above your circumstance and causing you to soar with the eagles? Your weakness is His strength! The paradigm of lives in Jody Amato's *Cinderella's Slipper* will gather your heap of ashes and bring forth a beautiful Bride for the King.

Pastor Darlene McCarty
Author and Speaker
Memphis, Tennessee

Introduction

Some might wonder why a Christian book would be entitled *Cinderella's Slipper*. It's a good question. Some periods of our lives have not always ended as we wished, and I believe that God wants to take some of us back, maybe even as far as our early childhood, in order to do a complete healing and restoration in us. His will is to make us complete in Him so that we can forget the drudgery and unfairness of the past and look forward to a bright and wonderful future.

In the eyes of God, we're all Cinderellas, and we all have a story to tell. We may not all have a wicked stepmother or two wicked stepsisters, but let's face it: life, for us, has been anything but a fairy tale. Life is tragically real, and so are the pains of heartbreak, betrayal and violation.

And let's not forget our own failures and mistakes. I don't know about you, but I can relate to all of the above.

But we didn't start life destined to live among the ashes and wear the rags of hopelessness and despair. The Word of God tells us that Jesus came to this earth to give us a wonderful life. He said:

My purpose is to give life in all its fullness.

John 10:10, NLT

So God didn't fail you. He didn't let you down—either as a child or as an adult.

But many people ask, "Why me? What did I do wrong that I deserved all of this?" Did you ever stop to think that maybe the things that have befallen you in life were not your fault? Jesus said something else in that same passage, something very important:

The thief's purpose is to steal and kill and destroy.

John 10:10, NLT

Maybe it's Satan who has tried to give you a guilt trip on top of all the heartbreak and disappointment you already feel.

You may have been in a relationship, and the next thing you knew the other person walked out, saying that it was "over." Someone you trusted betrayed you, and you still carry the guilt and shame of it. Things that happened to you as a small child seem to control your future and stifle any chance you have at happiness. And, like others, you may ask, "How could this happen to me? How could this happen to anyone?"

Well, I'll tell you. Before creation, a battle was already raging, a battle that even now continues. It was the battle between light and darkness, life and death, Heaven and Hell, God and Satan. The apostle Paul wrote to the early churches with this explanation:

> *For we are not fighting against people made of flesh and blood, but against the evil rulers and authorities of the unseen world, against those mighty powers of darkness who rule this world, and against wicked spirits in the heavenly realms. Use every piece of God's armor to resist the enemy in the time of evil, so that after the battle you will still be standing firm.*
>
> Ephesians 6:12-13, NLT

This explains it. Our battle is not with flesh and blood, but against evil rulers and authorities of the unseen world. Such powers gain control over and influence certain people. They cannot make them do something, for we all have a free will and can do good as well as evil. But some people are demon possessed and don't have the strength to fight alone the evil that controls them. In fact, without the help of Jesus, none of us can fight or control the power of our own flesh.

We're not talking about people foaming at the mouth and their head spinning around on their shoulders, so don't go running off to the video store to rent a video entitled: *How to Cast Out Demons, Part 1.* Some men of Paul's day tried that, and the demons turned on them and attacked them instead. They had seen Paul casting out demons and overheard him using the name of Jesus, so they tried the same thing. The result was not what they expected:

> But when they tried it on a man possessed by an evil spirit, the spirit replied, "I know Jesus, and I know Paul. But who are you?" And he leaped on them and attacked them with such violence that they fled from the house, naked and badly injured.   Acts 19:15-16, NLT

Demons are real forces of darkness, but don't believe for a minute that every problem you have is because someone is demon possessed. I take spiritual warfare very seriously, but we must find a balance. Jesus wants to uproot the cause of your pain—not just the symptoms (see Matthew 15:13). He wants you to be transformed, not just informed, by what He did at Calvary. He wants you to be aware of who and what is at the root of all your pain. Jesus can and will heal your broken heart, and He alone can dry your many tears.

This book was not written to tear down men. Ladies, there are many good men out there, men who have stood true and walked in love, only to have their hearts broken and their dreams torn apart by Satan working through some woman. This is a book about Cinderellas and the pain they bear. I want to start with some of the Cinderellas of the Bible, and as we walk through its pages and see the pain these women suffered, I'm convinced that we will also find a glass slipper for each one of them.

And just as there was a glass slipper that fit Cinderella's foot, I'm sure that one or more of the coming chapters will fit your life and circumstances, and I pray that you will allow the Holy Spirit to slip it on your foot in order to do a complete healing and restoration in you. Then you can finally find closure for some of those old wounds. Here, then, is *Cinderella's Slipper.*

Jody Amato
Walker, Louisiana

Chapter 1

Leah's Slipper

Now Laban had two daughters; the name of the older was Leah, and the name of the younger was Rachel. And Leah's eyes were weak, but Rachel was beautiful of form and face. ... Jacob loved Rachel.

Genesis 29:16-18, NAS

As we begin our journey through the books of the Bible to gaze upon the lives of some of the women of other ages and their struggles, I must stop first in the book of Genesis, and there I see the pain of Leah.

Leah Was Not in the "Beautiful" Category

Leah was one of two daughters of Laban. Their mother, sadly, had died. Leah, according to some ancient writings, may have been Rachel's twin, and yet the two were totally different. Leah was said to have dull or weak eyes. One writer said that she had no eyelashes. This is significant, for in those times a woman's eyes were a sign of her beauty. Therefore Leah could never be considered in that category.

I once knew a woman who had a nervous habit of pulling out her eyelashes. That might seem strange to some, but it's no more strange than biting one's fingernails. Nervous people have many strange habits. The bottom line is that Leah was considered to be plain, withdrawn and nervous.

On the other hand, her sister Rachel was said to be very beautiful, outgoing and full of laughter. So here was Leah, the eldest, or firstborn, single, always being overlooked by men and always being compared to her sister Rachel.

> *She held my face in her hands, looked deeply at me for a moment, and said, "My poor, poor little baby!"*

I Know What It Is

I know the pain of that. I know what it is to always be compared to others and always be considered the ugly one. I remember words my mother spoke over me as a small child that would set the stage for how I saw myself in the years to come.

She was fixing my hair one day. My bangs were uneven, my face was all freckled, and I had a big space between my front teeth. I'm sure she didn't think twice about what she said that day, and she had no idea that I would understand the significance of her words or that they would hurt me so deeply.

I'm sure Mama never meant to hurt me. Nevertheless, she spoke words into my life that day that would lay a foundation for how I would begin to picture myself. She held my face in her hands, looked deeply at me for a moment, and said, "My poor, poor little baby!" I was deeply hurt by that careless comment.

My mother was not the only one who did this. I also had an uncle who made unkind remarks about my looks, and there were others who openly referred to my sister Diane as "the pretty one." Satan cares nothing about innocent children, and he starts early trying to destroy them in any way he can.

You and I Must Be Very Careful with Our Words

You and I must be very careful about what we say to children, for they understand much more than we think. And words cut deep, whether they're spoken to a child, to an adolescent or to an adult. The greatest pain in life, next to losing someone you love through death, is having the person you love tell you they don't love you anymore, or they never did love you. Another is having a man tell you he can't marry you because you're unable to have children. But these are only two examples of the many lies that Satan uses to rip our hearts out of us. He is intent upon destroying our minds and our souls.

You might have been, or even now still are, in a relationship where you're constantly being compared to an ex-girlfriend or an ex-wife—how you look, how you dress, how you cook, how you clean and, yes, even the way you make love.

Some get compared to a neighbor, a relative, a friend, and let's not forget the mother-in-law. The list goes on and on, and so does the pain.

Making Us Feel "Less Than"

Isn't it just like Satan to try to make us feel "less than." Isn't he the father of lies? Hasn't he come to steal, kill and destroy? He robs us of our self-esteem, our self-worth, so that he can then kill our hope of ever being happy or of being good enough for anything in life. He wants to rob us of our joy, and he wants to destroy our dreams and visions for marriage, family and ministry.

Satan might be trying to make you feel "less than," but Jesus came to give you life and *"that more abundantly."* In other words, in the eyes of God, we are "more than" enough! Praise God for that.

The story of Leah and Rachel and Jacob is a familiar one to most of us, but if it's new to you, dear reader, I encourage you to read the book of Genesis and let the impact of this story bless your soul.

What Does Jacob Have to Do with It?

What does Jacob have to do with all this? He was the son of Isaac, who was the son of Abraham. Jacob's mother was Rebekah, who just happened to be the sister of Laban, the father of Leah and Rachel.

Jacob had been forced to flee from his father's home in fear for his life, for he had deceived his father and stolen his brother Esau's birthright. His mother told him to go to her family and to dwell there until things had cooled down at home, for Esau was so angry that he just might kill his brother.

Esau and Jacob were also twins, and some writings suggest that Esau should have, by the custom of the day, married Leah. But Esau was a free spirit who did what he wanted when he wanted, and he chose, instead, to marry a Hittite woman: Judith, the daughter of Beeri. In fact, Esau married two Hittite women. His other wife was Basemath, the daughter of Elon. Needless to say, this marriage outside of the family of faith brought many problems to Esau's family.

I Know What It Is To Marry Outside of the Faith

I, too, know what it is to marry outside the family of God. God, in His grace, can turn things around for us, but

that doesn't give any of us a license to marry an unbeliever. God's Word is very clear on this issue:

*Don't team up with those who are unbelievers. How
can goodness be a partner with wickedness? How can
light live with darkness? What harmony can there be
between Christ and the Devil? How can a believer be
a partner with an unbeliever? And what union can
there be between God's temple and idols? For we are
the temple of the living God. As God said:*

*"I will live in them
and walk among them.
I will be their God,
and they will be my people.
Therefore, come out from them
and separate yourselves from them, says the Lord.
Don't touch their filthy things,
and I will welcome you.
And I will be your Father,
and you will be my sons and daughters,
says the Lord Almighty."*

2 Corinthians 6:14-18, NLT

God's will is that we marry within the family of faith.
At the same time, this is not a reason to leave an unbe-
lieving spouse. "What, then, must we do?" some might
ask. When you find yourself in such a situation, God
requires you to walk in the fullness of love toward the

person you have been joined to—whether they walk in love or not. And as you do this, know that Jesus loves you and understands the great trial you're facing. He will help you. Your situation is not hopeless by any means, so trust Him to turn things around.

Now, let's get back to Leah.

Leah's Hope

If it's true that Esau would have been expected to marry Leah and didn't, then this represents another rejection for her, and it made Leah feel more ugly than ever and also alone and unwanted. She must have been told at a very young age that when she grew up she would marry Esau, and now he didn't want her. Was there to be no end to her misery?

But Jacob was coming her way. Maybe things would now turn in her favor.

Having left his father's home, Jacob made the arduous four-hundred-mile journey to the land of his mother, and there he came to

God requires you to walk in the fullness of love toward the person you have been joined to — whether they walk in love or not!

Laban's well. Within a short time, he had met Rachel, his cousin, and one glimpse of this beautiful woman told him that she was the woman of his dreams.

Jacob was soon invited to stay in his uncle's home, so he would have interacted with the whole family. I can't help but wonder what he thought when he first saw Leah, and I can't help but wonder what Leah felt when Rachel came running excitedly from the well to tell her father that she had met her cousin Jacob. Something tells me that Rachel confided in her sister that Jacob was very good looking and friendly—and single—and I'm sure she must have said it with a girlish giggle.

In that moment, Leah's heart must have leaped. Might Jacob be attracted to her? Was this possibly the man she had dreamed of for so long? Would he find her desirable? Would he rescue her from her nightmare existence? But when Jacob arrived, these hopes were quickly dashed, for it was now apparent to all that he had eyes only for Rachel. And poor Leah was rejected once again.

So In Love

Jacob was so in love with Rachel that he agreed to work for seven years for his uncle to earn her hand in marriage. And, amazingly, those seven years seemed to pass quickly. But when the seven years were accomplished, he was ready for his wife. He went to Laban to say that he had done his part, and now he expected to have his bride. Laban agreed, and the wedding was scheduled.

When the bride was brought into the celebration, she was heavily veiled. I don't know how much Jacob may have had to drink that day, but what we do know is that the veiled bride was not Rachel, and Jacob didn't even know it until the next morning. So that may be an indication that he'd had too much to drink.

Who Was This Bride?

And who was this bride? Leah had been convinced by her father that they were doing a good thing by posing her as Rachel and giving her in marriage to Jacob instead of her younger sister. How else could she get a husband? But what must it have been like to make love to a man who was in love with another woman and thought he was making love to her? During the night, Jacob must have whispered sweet nothings into Leah's ear, and all the while she knew that those words were not intended for her.

Poor Leah, all she wanted was to be loved. Was this the best she could hope for? Perhaps she clung to every word, trying to make each one her own. Maybe she decided that this was a good thing and would turn out for the best, as she fell asleep in the arms of the man she had been watching court her sister for the past seven years. Leah was a desperate woman, and she had resorted to desperate measures. She so longed to be loved, so longed for laughter and so longed for a family of her own.

Surely, after Jacob awoke the next morning and knew

the truth, he would be glad that Laban had tricked him, glad that he had given him Leah instead of Rachel. After all he had made love to her, and he had spent the whole night with her. In that moment, she had to trust that her father knew best. He had said that she was to be Jacob's wife and not Rachel, and now she had Jacob there with her in the dark.

> *We can all imagine how Jacob was feeling about then, but what about poor Leah?*

Waiting ... and for What?

So many good women have worked hard for the Kingdom of God as they waited, believing God for their proper mate to come. Pastors and prophets encouraged them to hold on, for their mate was surely coming, even indicating at times that they knew who the man was and, at others times, actually pointing him out. Because of this, the woman waited and worked for two long years, or four, or even six or nine years or more—only to discover one day that the man she had waited for all that time felt nothing at all for her.

This man didn't want her; he wanted someone else. This actually happened to me. What about you?

Jacob Was Furious

That next morning, when Jacob saw that his wife was not Rachel, but Leah, he was furious and went immediately to Laban to complain. Why had he cheated him so terribly?

We can all imagine how Jacob was feeling about then, but what about poor Leah? What must she have felt when she saw the look on her "husband's" face? It wasn't what she had expected or longed for, and it wasn't what she had made herself believe it would be. His face was contorted in anger, and his voice was filled with rage. The moment he had realized what they had done to him, he had jumped out of the bed, pulling away from her in horror and rushing out to find out why this thing had happened.

So there she was, all alone again—unloved, unwanted and now used. What could be worse?

Friend, maybe you've been in a relationship or just a one-night stand that you thought would be the beginning of something wonderful. It proved to be a lie, but sadly, because of your need to be loved, you bought into it. If you would just be willing to compromise your Christian testimony this once, you would surely find true love and the happiness you had longed for for so long. But, like Leah, the next morning you discovered just how wrong you had been. And this left you feeling deceived, used, hurt and very alone.

At Work to Destroy Your Mind

At this point, the enemy was at work to destroy Leah's mind. He's good at that.

One woman who was very close to me waited for nine years for a husband, only to wake up one morning two months after they were married and hear him say that he didn't love her and never had. She was so shocked in that moment that she fell back against the wall and slid down it to the floor.

Somewhere in this process, she soiled her pants, but her immediate response was to get up and start cleaning the bathtub. She was, for the moment, unaware of the fact that her bowels had been involuntarily released. Her mind was simply unable to process the reality of the words she had just heard with her ears, and the effect it had on her was terrible.

I'm sure that Leah's mind was spinning out of control. She was remembering each moment of their time together, how he had held her, how he had kissed her, the things he had said. Surely he could not have been so naive as to think that it was really Rachel. Surely he had known and made love to her anyway. Or, at least, that's what her mind had allowed her to believe or had allowed her to hope. Now what?

What Anguish, Pain and Rejection!

What anguish, pain and rejection Leah must have felt

when see saw the look on Jacob's face and heard his voice so full of anger and contempt! And part of it was being directed at her. Yes, Jacob was angry with Laban for having tricked him, but he was also angry with Leah for agreeing to the whole situation. He was angry that she was not Rachel, for he loved Rachel and had sacrificed many good years to make her his own.

Feeling him jerk away from her in such a rage and with such resentment, as if she had done something unforgivable, must have been unbearable for Leah. She must have been at a loss to understand it. In her mind, she had only done what her father had urged her to do. What was her great sin?

Before we go any further, let me insert this important point: God will never tell you to lie to or deceive others, and if anyone tells you differently, then the truth is not found in them. How many hearts have been broken, and how many lives have been destroyed because someone felt lost and alone, and they believed the lie of Satan and acted upon it? Don't you ever be guilty of such lies.

A Week to Win Jacob's Love

Laban agreed, after Jacob had confronted him, to give him Rachel as a second wife, but he would have to work another seven years for her, and he would also have to fulfill his wedding week with Leah first—for this was absolutely required by the law and the customs of the day. Now Leah had a whole week to win Jacob's love—or a week to think about him wanting to be with someone else. As he lay with her in body, his heart was really somewhere else. To Leah, this must have felt like a marriage made in Hell, instead of one made in Heaven.

I know what it is to have people you trust and respect tell you that a certain man was destined by God to be your mate, only to find after the marriage that the man actually loved and wanted someone else. Oh, yes, I know that pain very well. Within two weeks after our marriage, my "husband" was back seeing his ex-wife.

I hadn't known them when they were together, so it had been no problem for me to open my heart to her and not perceive her as a threat to our marriage. After all, this was God's choice for my mate—or so I was told. When I learned that he was still in love with her, the pain of it was unbearable.

I can remember asking Jesus, just before I went to sleep one night, "Please don't let me wake up in the morning." But, by His grace, I did wake up, and by His grace, I was delivered from the torments of Hell.

These are hard lessons to learn. Not all mates are sent to us by God, and as believers, we need to fast and pray to find His perfect will for our lives. He does confirm His Word—when we give Him a chance. If you're contemplating marriage, take time to get to know the other person. God's Word shows us that we're not to simply accept people for what they say; we must also test their spirits:

Beloved, believe not every spirit, but try the spirits whether they are of God: because many false prophets are gone out into the world.

1 John 4:1

God will not leave you in ignorance. I knew, by the things I was seeing and hearing, that something was wrong, but I chose to ignore it all because I wanted to believe that this man loved me. I certainly wanted him. This demonstrates very powerfully our need to seek the Lord before we put our hearts at risk, and we must never put our bodies at risk. I later realized that, time and time again, the Lord had been trying to show me that this man wanted someone else. Why had I not heeded these warnings? The answer is probably that I was desperate for love.

Later, I asked the man, "Then why did you marry me?"

He said, "I didn't want to lose you before I knew what I really wanted." I had been used, and it was nobody's fault but my own. Sometimes we don't re-

> *I can remember asking Jesus, just before I went to sleep one night, "Please don't let me wake up in the morning!"*

ally want to see the truth, and so we have to bear the consequences.

No Give and Take

Has someone you loved left you for someone else? Did you pour your whole heart into trying to please some man, trying to win his love, but to no avail? Leah tried hard to please Jacob. She gave him six sons, and she was sure that this would win his undying devotion. She said:

> *Surely the LORD hath looked upon my affliction; now therefore my husband will love me.*
>
> Genesis 29:32, KJV

But there was no give and take in this marriage. Leah had to do all the giving, and still she was forced to endure the constant pain of watching Jacob find joy and laughter in the arms of another women. I know what that's like, seeing your husband walking, joking and flirting with someone else, knowing in your heart that he wants her and yet not daring to say a word about it until it's too late.

Like Leah, many women think that if they can just have a child with their man or if they can somehow buy a house together, then a more stable bond will develop between them, and they will find happiness together. But don't confuse bonds with love. I once had a strong bond with a sports car I owned, but I assure you it wasn't true love or commitment. When I felt it was the right time and I needed the money, I sold the car. No physical bond is sufficient to hold a marriage together. Love and commitment is and always will be the only thing that can do that.

And it takes two. Both of you have to be committed to the relationship, and both of you need God's love. And, of course, true love leads to commitment.

You can be committed to God only when you truly love Him. And when you no longer feel love for your spouse, your commitment to Jesus will keep you committed to the marriage. Honey, the truth is that your love is not as dead as you might think it is. It's just buried underneath all of the hurts, the disappointments and the broken promises. But Jesus can and will restore, or awaken, that love again, as we forgive each other and reach out to each other. So once the commitment is there, storms can come against you, and you'll stand.

Jacob and Leah had only a physical commitment. She stayed with him, and he did his duty to her as a husband, but she wanted his heart, and that was owned by another woman.

You Did It All

Some women can say that they did it all. They waited on their man hand and foot—ironing his clothes, running his bath water, laying out his towels and what he was to wear the next day. They even ran to meet him at the door when he came home each evening. And that's just

> *Satan*
> *may*
> *be*
> *telling*
> *you*
> *that*
> *you*
> *can't*
> *get*
> *a*
> *man*
> *and*
> *keep*
> *him*
> *because*
> *you're*
> *too*
> *old,*
> *too*
> *fat,*
> *too*
> *plain,*
> *too*
> *tall*
> *or*
> *too*
> *short!*

the beginning of their list. But it still wasn't enough. I know. I did it all too. And yet the more I loved, the more I seemed to be unloved.

When I was abandoned, I complained about it all one night to the Lord, and He answered me: "Yet shall you continue to love." He led me to open the Bible, and it fell open to Paul's words to the Corinthians. They were exactly what I had just said to the Lord:

And I will very gladly spend and be spent for you; though the more abundantly I love you, the less I be loved.   2 Corinthians 12:15

Then the Lord said, "It is the love you gave that will bring him back. He's missing your love." And sure enough he came and said that he was missing my love and wanted to come back. It lasted for a time.

You Can't Get a Man

Satan may be telling you that you can't get a man and keep him because you're too old, too fat, too plain, too tall, too short, too dark or too light. Always keep in mind that he is the *"father of lies"*:

> *He was a murderer from the beginning and has always hated the truth. There is no truth in him. When he lies, it is consistent with his character; for he is a liar and the father of lies.* John 8:44, NLT

When your true mate comes along, he'll be looking at the spirit, not the flesh, so you have nothing to worry about.

Please don't misunderstand me. We should do our best with what God has given us, always looking as nice as possible and taking care of our bodies.

And I'm not saying that God will or will not bring someone back into your life. What I'm saying is what Jesus said:

> *I reap where I sowed not, and gather where I have not strawed.* Matthew 25:26

If you have planted love, trust, compassion, mercy (and please don't forget forgiveness), you will reap from that seed—if not in that particular field, then in another. Honey, believe me, you will find true love.

In time, Jacob came to realize that Leah was from the Lord, and also that she was for him. Rachel died young, and then Jacob and Leah had many more years to grow old together. So there's hope for you too.

If the Shoe Fits ...

If Leah's slipper fits your foot today, allow the Holy Spirit to set you free from the pain, torment and heartbreak of your past. When we have Jesus, we don't have to look to our past anymore, and we can have a glorious future full of His great love.

Amen!

Chapter 2

Rachel's Slipper

Laban said, "Complete the week of this one, and we will give you the other also for the service which you shall serve with me for another seven years." Jacob did so and completed her week, and he gave him his daughter Rachel as his wife. Genesis 29:26-28, NAS

We already know Rachel. She was Leah's sister and, perhaps, her twin. She was very beautiful, and she was said to be outgoing and full of life. Because of that, her days seemed to be filled with joy and laughter.

Rachel was the shepherdess in the family, and we first encounter her at the well watering her father's flocks. Since Rachel was the youngest daughter (perhaps only by mere minutes), this task fell to her. It was during one of her trips to the well to water the sheep that something wonderful happened to her, and that is often the case with us as well.

The Appointed Day

I'm sure that this day must have seemed like all other days to Rachel, as she started out on a task she had repeated so often before. She was dedicated to her father's business, but watering sheep didn't seem like a very romantic thing to be doing for a young lady of marriageable age. Probably she never dreamed that she was about to meet the love of her life at the well.

He was, of course, Jacob, son of Isaac, and it was love at first sight. She would love him, and he would love her—with all his heart. It was a love so deep that he was willing to work fourteen years to gain her hand in marriage.

At most any age, being single and wondering just when your proper mate will come along can be one of the most disappointing and frustrating things any woman can face in life. But if we will just do as Rachel did, go about our Father's business, we will eventually meet our man— perhaps just when and where we least expect it.

Aunt Rebekah's Experience

Rachel's Aunt Rebekah had a very similar experience when she was young. She also went to the well, this time with a water jug on her shoulder, and there she met a man known as Eliezer of Damascus. Eliezer was the servant of Abraham, and Abraham had sent him to find a suitable wife for his son Isaac. Believe me, just as Abraham sent his servant Eliezer, God will send the Holy Spirit to seek out and locate your perfect mate.

Once located, the Holy Spirit will test the man's heart to see if he is chaste and committed to God and to His Word. This is an important process, for you don't want to be deceived and end up living with a whoremonger, and neither does your mate. So take time to test the spirits beforehand.

Eliezer prayed and asked the Lord to cause the young woman He had chosen specifically for his master's son to offer to give him something to drink, and also to offer to water his camels. And that's exactly what Rebekah did, for God had chosen her.

Oh, beloved, seek God before you think about giving your heart away. If you don't, the man you're kissing may be destined by God to

I'm sure that this day must have seemed like all other days to Rachel, as she started out on a task she had repeated so often before!

be someone else's husband. Protect the men you meet, and ask God to place the same type of woman in your mate's path, one who will guard his heart and his virginity until it's time for you to go to the well.

If you keep your eyes on Jesus, the living water, and go about your Father's business, you will get your answer. Jesus said it this way:

> *But seek ye first the kingdom of God, and his righteousness; and all these things shall be added unto you.*
> Matthew 6:33

If you do this, I assure you that you will find your God-ordained mate, and don't let anyone tell you differently. Refuse to entertain any doubts. Just believe.

It is God's will for you to be married. Way back at the beginning He said:

> *It is not good that the man should be alone; I will make him an help meet for him.* Genesis 2:18

And God hasn't change His mind about marriage. So, marriage is not your idea; it's God's. He ordained marriage in His Word, and His Word will never *"return ... void"*:

> *So shall my word be that goeth forth out of my mouth: it shall not return unto me void, but it shall accom-*

plish that which I please, and it shall prosper in the thing whereto I sent it. Isaiah 55:11

Walking on Cloud Nine

It all happened so quickly, and now Rachel knew who she would spend the rest of her life with. The marriage would not take place soon, for Jacob had agreed to work for her father for seven years to gain her. But that thought only heightened her excitement.

This man loved her, and he loved her a lot. For the next seven years, she was walking on cloud nine, dreaming of her wedding night.

It was all so wonderful! The seven years passed in a whirlwind of excitement. Then what seemed so wonderful suddenly turned into a terrible nightmare.

The Dream Turns Nightmare

Where was Rachel when it came time for the wedding? Almost certainly she had to be hidden away somewhere, for Laban and Leah could not risk letting her spoil their plans. Did she know what was about to happen? She had to have known something. At the very least, she knew that a wedding was going on and she was not there. She must have either known or suspected the treachery that was being carried out behind her back.

Did she witness any of the actual ceremony? Did she see another woman standing in her place? Did she see

> *I know the pain of sitting up at night waiting for a husband to come home, yet knowing in my heart that he was in bed with another woman!*

another woman being taken to the bridal tent to lie with Jacob?

One consolation for Rachel is that Jacob was not part of this treachery. Many godly women have stood in the gap for their man, believing God to change him and restore the love they once shared, only to have him suddenly divorce her and quickly marry another.

Whatever happens, don't allow Satan to harm your faith in the Most High God. David, in the Psalms, made this statement:

For the LORD God is a sun and shield: the LORD will give grace and glory: no good thing will he withhold from them that walk uprightly. Psalm 84:11

Jesus feels your pain, and if He hasn't brought your man back, it's because He has something better for you. You're a miracle looking for a place to happen, so open your heart in faith, and let that miracle begin today.

How Did Rachel Feel?

Nothing is recorded about exactly how Rachel felt when all of this happened or what she said, but I can tell you from experience that she must have been emotionally devastated. To know that your man, the man God Himself picked for you and miraculously united you with, the man you love more than anyone else in this world, has been joined in marriage to another woman and that he is, at that very moment, spending the night with her ... words simply cannot express the pain of it all.

I know the pain of sitting up at night waiting for a husband to come home, praying that he was safe and yet knowing in my heart that he was in bed with another woman. I told myself that I was wrong for wanting to believe anything but the painful truth, as I watched the clock tick away on my broken heart. Then the phone rang, and a friend was on the line to confirm my worst fears and tell me where he was.

Next, I ran and jumped in the car and started off to find him, praying the whole time that it was not true. Then I was there, banging on the door, and when the door finally opened, there stood my life before me.

But he didn't have the look of sorrow or shame I expected. Instead, he was angry, and we argued. He looked at my tear-stained face and said, "If you were home where you belong, we wouldn't be having this argument." The saddest thing is that Satan had "done such a number" on my mind that for a moment I actually believed him.

I took a deep breath, and inside I was silently crying to God for this man to take me in his arms and tell me everything was okay. Anything to make the pain go away. At that point, I would have believed almost anything that enabled me to dry my eyes for a moment. I could read into what he was saying things he didn't really mean. Whatever he said sounded to me like, "I didn't really mean it. It's you I love and want and no other." But, of course, it didn't really happen. So instead, I was dying on the inside, and the hurt and anger were more than I felt I could bear.

Think of It!

Think of it! Although Jacob protested and declared his love for Rachel and his desire to still have her as his wife, she had to sit back and watch for a whole week while he fulfilled his marital duty to Leah. Even though he had been deceived, he was still expected to obey the laws and customs of the day. And for Rachel, those nights, knowing he was making love to someone else, had to be inexpressibly bitter.

Next, Rachel had to face a new challenge. She was soon to be married to this man, who was even now on a honeymoon with another woman. What would their first night together be like? In her mind, no doubt, she wondered: Would Jacob find her as desirable as he did Leah? Would she be able to please him as her sister had? Would he think about Leah when he made love to her?

She had certainly been betrayed by her father and her sister, but did she also feel betrayed by this man who said he loved her and then went to someone else's bed? Betrayal cuts deep. Fortunately for us, Jesus knew that kind of pain in His own life, so He understands what we're going through. I also know that God is a restorer. Jesus came that we might have life and have it more abundantly, and that means restoration from what we are to what He can make of us.

At one point, I asked God how I could ever trust again. Then the Lord spoke to me in a very tender voice these words that are still written upon my heart: "Jody, you will trust a man again when you learn to trust Me again." Honey, the peace of mind that we each so desperately need today will come when we're able to trust God with all our tomorrows. Man may hurt you, but God never will.

If the Shoe Fits ...

So even Rachel had a story to tell, and if her slipper fits you today, allow Jesus (for He is the Healer and the healing water, a never-drying well) to take control of your life. Come into His presence today and allow the Holy Spirit to fill you and touch your broken heart. He can make you whole again. Not only can He, but He *will.*

Amen!

Chapter 3

Abigail's Slipper

The woman was intelligent and beautiful in appearance, but the man was harsh and evil in his dealings.
1 Samuel 25:3, NAS

As we continue on our journey, we stop to peer through the window of the heart of a woman named Abigail. She was said to be both a woman of good understanding and very beautiful. Some of us would think that Abigail surely had it made, being married to a man who had money, a man of wealth. His name was Nabal. It also appears, however, that he was a man given to hard drinking, an evil man, harsh with his actions and with his words.

The story is found in the book of 1 Samuel, and the Bible makes clear that Abigail was what Proverbs calls *"a virtuous woman"* (Proverbs 31:10), a woman of great commitment and integrity. In the same way, you may be standing for the things of Christ, and like this woman, you're willing to pay a great price to fulfil the vows you've made in life—not only to marriage, but also to the ministry to which the Lord God has called you. If so, learn from Abigail.

> *You may be in the type of relationship where you have to make constant excuses for someone else's bad behavior!*

David's Request

One day David sent some messengers to Nabal to request food for himself and his men. It was shearing season, and the custom of the time was that anyone who took part in the herding, protection or shearing of the animals was entitled to partake of the feast that followed. David and his men were camped out in the fields around Nabal's land, and they, therefore, served as a wall of protection around his herds. During that time, they never confiscated any of the animals, so David was within his rights when he asked the man for food.

Some of you are tending to a brother's field, praying the prayer of faith over it and serving as protection for him and his. And don't stop praying, beloved. Your day of reward is coming. Because of our covenant with Father God, you're guaranteed a portion of the upcoming Great Feast (that all the money in the world can't buy a ticket to), and it's nearly time for the shearing.

Nabal Was Evil

But Nabal was evil, and he turned down the request of David and refused to send anything back with his men—other than insults. Needless to say, David was very angry when he heard this report. This insult was so grievous that he determined to return to Nabal's house and to destroy him and his men.

Fortunately, Abigail had more sense than her evil husband. When one of Nabal's servants told her what the master had said to David's messengers, after all the good David had done to protect the flocks, she knew what she must do. Concerned about what would happen to her household if nothing was done to correct this offense, she set about to do just that.

Constantly Making Excuses for Abusive Behavior

You may know how Abigail felt that day, for you may be in the type of relationship where you have to make constant excuses for someone else's abusive behavior. You have to think of something to say to your children, to other family members, to friends, to neighbors and even to strangers, because your husband (or your father, mother, son or daughter) is drunk or on drugs again. You may feel that you have to lie to cover up the verbal abuse, or even physical abuse, you're suffering. Or you may be fearful for some other loved one who is suffering in this way.

I know what it is to fear for a loved one who is sitting in a hospital emergency room after jumping out of a truck going forty-five miles an hour. She was trying to escape the physical abuse she was suffering at the hand of the man driving the truck. It is so sad that Satan can inflict this much pain on a human being that jumping from a moving truck would seem safer than continuing to suffer abuse from another human being.

I Know What It Is

I know what it is to live with an alcoholic father, to watch him drag my Mom out of bed in the middle of the night. I know what it is to run outside screaming for someone to help. But no one would hear or answer the screams of a six-year-old girl who thought her Mama was being killed.

I know the shame of having your clothes ripped off and then being pushed out the front door and having the door locked behind you. There I was standing, naked, crying, pleading, asking for forgiveness for something I hadn't done ... anything to get back in that door, so that no one else would see my shame.

Satan has a field day ripping lives apart, and it's not just the grown-ups who suffer. It's also the children standing in the background, listening through the door or peeking through the cracks. Even worse, many times the children are the victims, the actual targets of the abuse.

Are You a Target?

Were you or are you, even now, the target of such bad behavior? If so, have you been left alone to feel the pain and fear of living in a Hell-house of torment, where such a demon reigns? If so, then please read on. I know Someone who can help you. He served an eviction notice on Satan, telling him to get out. And He's about to pour the balm of Gilead out upon your life today.

His name is Jesus Christ, and if Satan is telling you that it's Friday (the day of Christ's suffering and death), tell him that he's looking at the wrong calendar. It's not Friday at all. It's Sunday (the day of Christ's resurrection), and the work of Christ on the cross is complete. And He did it all for you.

Abigail Took Things into Her Own Hands

Abigail told a servant to pack some supplies of food and wine. She was going out to meet David—at the risk of her own life. And, sure enough, she met David in the way. He was on his way to take vengeance upon Nabal.

In this way, Abigail stood in the gap for her household and, yes, even for the wicked Nabal.

If you're in an abusive relationship, I can't tell you either to stay or to go. What I can tell you is that you must intercede in prayer for that abusive person, for they are being controlled by demons.

Some of you know what it is to stand in the gap for your marriage and to give all that you have and more. You fought every demon in Hell—only to see your marriage fail. You now feel like you lost the battle, but that's not the case. The Word of God declares that the battle belongs to the Lord. David himself said it the day he faced the giant Goliath:

And all this assembly shall know that the LORD saveth not with sword and spear: for the battle is the LORD's, and he will give you into our hands. 1 Samuel 17:47

And since the battle is the Lord's and He never loses a battle, the victory is His too.

Your battle may be going in a different direction than you imagined it would, but don't despair. Jesus won everything for us at Calvary, so never allow Satan to tell you anything different. The victory is ours. We just have to start walking in it.

Nabal Didn't Change

Abigail stood in the gap and risked her own life to

save her family (including her evil husband), and after all that, Nabal still didn't change. God then took things into His own hands and physically removed Nabal from her life.

Sometimes God removes people from our lives, and when He does, it's always for a good reason. He wants to spare our hearts and to save our minds. And let's not forget our souls.

In time, David heard that Abigail had been left single, and he sent for her and made her his own wife.

If the Shoe Fits ...

Maybe Abigail's slipper fits you today. If so, remember, we always reap what we sow. I know that you have sowed with all your heart, soul and mind, and Jesus knows it too. Sometimes we reap in a field we haven't even planted in. Abigail stood in the gap for a man who was lost, and God gave her a king in return.

Amen!

Chapter 4

Bathsheba's Slipper

The woman conceived; and she sent and told David, and said, "I am pregnant."   2 Samuel 11:5, NAS

As we stroll through the book of 2 Samuel, we encounter a woman who was said to be very lovely, and she was bathing one evening in some type of outdoor area where she was seen by King David from his quarters. Her name was Bathsheba, and her husband's name was Uriah. He was a soldier in David's army that was, at that very moment, off doing battle.

David and Bathsheba

The story of David and Bathsheba is one of the best known stories of the Bible. When David saw Bathsheba

57

bathing that night, he desired her. Unfortunately, he acted upon his urges, sending for her and lying with her. Later, Bathsheba discovered that she was pregnant with David's child, and she went and told him.

Satan comes as a thief in the night to steal from the purity of a marriage bed. Maybe you have found yourself, at some point, in bed with someone you weren't married to or even pregnant and not married to the father of your baby. If so, you've surely found yourself in the midst of a lot of pain, and I'm sure that Satan had a field day tormenting your mind because of it. All of this on top of the guilt and shame you already felt.

Isn't it good to know that God's grace and mercy are available to all of us? If we repent of our sins, Jesus casts them into the sea of forgetfulness. If someone is tearing you down, it's Satan. It's surely not God.

The Cover-up

David didn't need any scandals in his kingdom, so he decided to try to cover up this sin. If it became known that Bathsheba was bearing his child, she could even be stoned to death. He sent for Uriah, thinking to send him home to sleep with his wife. Then it might appear to everyone that the child was his.

Maybe you have become pregnant by someone you loved, only to have them say something that gripped your spirit and tore your heart to pieces. "Oh, who's the father?

This child can't be mine." In that moment, your heart and mind felt the pain of rejection. How could such words come out of the same mouth that said, "I love you," and "I will love you forever"?

Some men have drunk from this bitter cup too. They loved a woman with all their heart, only to be told by her that the child she was carrying was not theirs. It belonged to another man. This kind of heartbreak knows no gender bias and no age discrimination. Satan could care less if you're ninety or just twelve. It is so sad to see people of any age destroyed and their visions and dreams fallen to the ground.

> *Satan comes as a thief in the night to steal from the purity of a marriage bed!*

Uriah Didn't Cooperate

Uriah didn't do as David had hoped. The next day he reported to David that because his men were sleeping in the open field and preparing to continue the battle the next morning, it just wouldn't have been right for him to go home and sleep with his wife. Some men (and now some women) get so busy trying to impress their boss that they fail to meet the legitimate needs of their mate.

Because Uriah was such a dedicated army man, this must have happened to Bathsheba often through the years. Surely Uriah could have spent more time with her rather than with his job or with his fellow soldiers.

Forced?

When Bathsheba's original encounter with King David occurred, the King James Version of the Bible declares:

And David sent messengers, and took her.

2 Samuel 11:4

The use of this word *"took"* sounds like it was done by force. Many women know what it is to be forced against their will.

Some women are forced to stay home and watch the children, after they have starched and ironed their husbands clothes, so that he can go out with the guys to bars or clubs. I know this to be true. Sometimes it's worse. He's actually going out to meet another woman.

I can remember feeling so weak from sickness that I prayed for Jesus to give me the strength to iron my husband's cloths. He would tell his friends, "She likes me to look pretty." And that was true. I did like him to look pretty. I was very proud. But I didn't want to iron his clothes, only to have him use them to impress someone else.

Sometimes Satan sends his messenger of lies, and you find yourself left feeling all alone, just watching the clock, waiting for your man to come home, so that you can hear the voice of an adult. You're very lonely for someone to talk to.

It's not always about feeling the need for sex. Often it's about being alone in a bed made for two. Sometimes we just need to feel some loving arms reaching out to us and then holding us.

Satan uses lies to force you to think thoughts you never knew you would have, and in some cases to do things you now regret. He uses pride, selfishness and lust to project loneliness and rejection, and all the while he is setting a trap of destruction for your life and the life of those around you.

Whether you're a man or a woman, you will be crushed sooner are later by the hand of the enemy if you let him have his way. Then you will find yourself without any peace, and what you have done will bring about some type of death—whether spiritual, physical or emotional. A marriage can die, and so can a child's dream of a family that will always be together.

Ending a Marriage

Maybe you, at some point, made the decision to end a marriage, and you know what conflicting feelings that decision can bring. Think about Bathsheba. I wonder if she spent some nights in regret, longing to return to the arms of her first husband and yet knowing that it was now too late. I wonder if she felt, like most do, that part of her was missing.

> *I was in a relationship once in which I was so eaten up with fear that it would fail that my fears led me to end it prematurely!*

There's something about a first marriage. You imagine that it will last forever, and suddenly forever has come and gone, and you're all alone. If it happened to you, do you now feel trapped with no way out? Does fear, depression and anxiety try to take hold of you? Do you feel a deep frustration that somehow you can't turn the clock back and recapture the happiness you once enjoyed? Our God wants to reach out to you today and turn your life around.

Causing Your Own Failure

I was in a relationship once in which I was so eaten up with fear that it would fail that my fears led me to end it prematurely. I had totally convinced myself that it would end anyway. I can remember, in those moments, crying out for someone, anyone, to tell me that this marriage would last. Because I didn't hear it, I ended it myself.

King Saul often comes to my mind when I think about our self-destructive tendencies. He was the first appointed king over Israel, and he seemed to have it all ... until the enemy came along and caused him to take his eyes off of God. Saul ended up destroying the very thing he was trying to save.

In his case, it was a kingdom, while, in ours, it's a marriage. I destroyed a perfectly good relationship because of fear of the unknown. Anxiety came in and controlled my every thought, and this caused my confusion.

This battle, as with many of us, was in my mind, and it was a battle to the death. When it happens, some can go back, and some can't. If you would have to do something wrong to go back, then maybe you should think long and hard about trying it. Pray and ask God what He would have you to do, always remembering that two wrongs never make a right.

Drunkenness

Because Uriah slept in the courtyard that night, the next night David decided to get him drunk so that he would go home to his wife. Before I made Jesus Lord of my life, I spent a great deal of time in night clubs. I was a people watcher, and I saw and spoke with more than a few men who stopped off after work to have a drink with their boss during happy hour and walked out the door hours later with a strange woman on their arm. Some said they really hadn't wanted to come there, but they did it because their boss went.

I remember one man who started coming often. He said he just loved to dance. I asked him if he was married, and he said he was. What came out of my mouth next still rings in my ears today. I said, "Well, if you keep coming here, you won't be married for long." In that moment, a great sadness filled my heart.

Then it turned to anger, as he tried to defend his actions. "My wife doesn't mind," he said. "She doesn't like to dance." It wasn't very long before that man suddenly found himself single again. Real men and women go home at night to their families. Uriah still didn't go home that night, and the next day he returned to the battlefield.

Repentance Is the Route to Recovery

Instead of David going to God and repenting of his sin, he was trying to cover it up. And the only way we can cover sin (in our own efforts) is with more sin. Whatever we do to try to hide sin, it will remain hidden for only a short season. Our Lord tells us that whatever is hidden will be brought to light:

> *The Lord ... will bring to light the hidden things of darkness, and will make manifest the counsels of the hearts.* 1 Corinthians 4:5

Now David was getting desperate, and he did a desperate and despicable thing. He ordered Uriah to be placed in the worst part of the battle so that he would be killed. It's amazing the lengths we will sometimes go to cover up sin, rather than simply repenting of it and allowing God to wash us clean with the blood of His Son Jesus Christ.

Face it, we must each reap what we sow. Why does that have to be the case? Can't we escape punishment if we're sorry enough? No, because God is God, and His Word is sure. That Word tells us that He chastises those whom He loves:

> *So you should realize that just as a parent disciplines a child, the LORD your God disciplines you to help you.* Deuteronomy 8:5, NLT

> *And you have forgotten the exhortation which speaks to you as to sons:*

> *"My son, do not despise the chastening of the LORD,*
> *Nor be discouraged when you are rebuked by Him;*
> *For whom the LORD loves He chastens,*
> *And scourges every son whom He receives."*
> *If you endure chastening, God deals with you as with sons; for what son is there whom a father does not chasten? But if you are without chastening, of which all have become partakers, then you are illegitimate and not sons.* Hebrews 12:5-8, NKJ

Being chastised by God is not a bad thing. He's doing it because He loves you, and you can learn by it.

Those Who Wrong You Will Also Suffer

In the same way, those who wrong you will also suffer. If anyone has hurt you unjustly and caused you pain and grief, the judgment of the Lord will come upon them— even though God loves them. They will never go unpunished. God tells us emphatically:

> *Dearly beloved, avenge not yourselves, but rather give place unto wrath: for it is written, Vengeance is mine; I will repay, saith the Lord. Therefore if thine enemy hunger, feed him; if he thirst, give him drink: for in so doing thou shalt heap coals of fire on his head. Be not overcome of evil, but overcome evil with good.*
>
> Romans 12:19-21

When someone hurts you, he or she is hurting the Lord. It may, at times, look like nothing is happening to them, but just look at what happened to David. He had Uriah killed, and he then married Bathsheba. This accomplished, since she was carrying his child, everything seemed to be finished and forgotten. But nothing could be further from the truth.

God Sent Nathan

Just when it seemed that everything was going well, the Lord sent Nathan the prophet to confront David for his wrong. Using a sort of fable, Nathan quickly exposed everything that was thought to be hidden and forgotten. And, through Nathan, the Lord spoke forth His judgment for this sin. The child Bathsheba was carrying would die.

We don't have to wait until we die for judgment to come upon us. It comes when we least expect it. So if someone has ripped your heart out, God's judgment will surely come upon them—even if they happen to be in ministry.

David was God's chosen, anointed and appointed king over His people, but that didn't stop judgment from coming to him. Just as Nathan had said, the child died. And it was David and Bathsheba who made the decision that caused the death of that child.

Maybe you, too, made a mistake that caused someone to die. Maybe that mistake was an abortion. If so, then you've fought with demons of guilt and shame for years. Maybe you suffered a miscarriage, and still you've fought within yourself over anything you might have done that caused it. What's sure is that the enemy always tells you that you caused the death of your child—whether it's true or not.

> *David was God's chosen, anointed and appointed king over His people, but that didn't stop judgment from coming to him!*

Miscarriages in Ministry

Suffering a miscarriage can mean more than losing a natural child. You can have a miscarriage of your ministry, your vision, your dream. In many cases, wrong decisions have caused us to miscarry, or to abort, a ministry given to us by God. But just because we walked in disobedience once doesn't eliminate us from the race. God is still the God of the second chance.

Think about it. God not only allowed Bathsheba to conceive a second child by David, but this child, whose name was Solomon, was chosen by God to be the next king of Israel and to build the great Temple of the Lord in Jerusalem where the holy Ark of His presence would dwell. Oh, isn't God good!

If the Shoe Fits ...

If Bathsheba's slipper fits your foot, if you have done wrong and been wronged by others, the Lord Jesus is faithful today to forgive. He can rebuild your life and impregnate you with a new vision and dream. Let Him wash away all the guilt and shame you have suffered for playing a part in an abortion or the guilt of someone else's death, and trust Him that He is the God of new beginning and restoration. Welcome the Holy Spirit today to slip the healing power of Jesus Christ, not only onto your foot, but over your whole life and the lives of those around you.

Amen!

Chapter 5

Tamar's Slipper

*He took hold of her and said to her, "Come, lie with
me, my sister."*
*But she answered him, "No, my brother, do not violate
me; ... do not do this disgraceful thing!"*
*He would not listen to her; since he was stronger than
she, he violated her and lay with her.*

2 Samuel 13:11-12 and 14, NAS

As we move on in the sacred Scriptures, the stories of
the lives of women of every age march past us. We must
not overlook the children and especially the daughters.

Children are often the victims of intense pain and
abuse, so intense that the years that come often cannot
and will not erase it from their memories. It tears apart,
not only their little hearts, but also their little minds. This
story may speak to you.

David's Daughter and Amnon's Half-Sister

Tamar was the daughter of King David, the sister of Absalom and the half-sister of Amnon. Unfortunately, Amnon felt what we call "unnatural love" for her. This was an unhealthy and unlawful lust for his sister. Poor little Tamar was totally innocent, a young virgin who had her whole life ahead of her, and she certainly didn't need any distractions like this. But Amnon became so obsessed with his desire for her that it made him physically ill.

> *Tamar begged Amnon not to do this horrible thing to her, but he wouldn't listen to her pitiful pleas!*

As I read this story, I can somehow feel how devastated Satan feels at the very thought of us coming to Christ and becoming pure through the washing of His blood. It makes him sick. In Christ, we become part of His sweet, pure Bride. And just as sin is a stench in the nostrils of God, purity is a stench to Satan. When he sees it, he shrinks back in utter agony. Praise God for that.

I'm sure that Tamar, at her age, was dreaming of her future, her wedding, her bridegroom and their life together. What pretty things she would wear on that special day and how beautiful everything would be! She was pure, until this terrible enemy came in, and then her life was suddenly destroyed by this person she loved and trusted — a family member. Who would ever dream that someone in your own family would do such a terrible thing to an innocent child?

Pretending to Be Sick

Amnon went about his treachery very methodically. Pretending to be sick, he asked that Tamar be allowed to come to his room and prepare him some honey cakes to make him feel better. Oh, how deceptive and sly Satan is! When everything seems to be conspiring against you, you can know that he is behind it all.

Tamar was very trusting, and so, never imagining that her brother had something bad in mind, she brought the cakes he had asked for. In that moment, he grabbed her and forced her to have sex with him.

Tamar begged Amnon not to do this horrible thing to her, but he wouldn't listen to her pitiful pleas. He was so obsessed with his own desires that nothing and no one could dissuade him. He carried out his fantasies upon his little sister that day.

Some Jewish scholars have written that Tamar was raped repeatedly and that some of the sex acts performed on her were very unnatural and very disgusting. How terrible!

Molested in Childhood

One day a woman in her early forties unexpectedly appeared at my door. She first introduced herself, and then what she said next came as a complete surprise. Without blinking an eye, she said to me, "I was molested when I was a very small child." I stood there for a brief moment, unsure of what to say or not say, and then I invited her in, and we talked for a while. Over the years, she had gone from man to man, running from her pain. Because of her childhood experiences, she thought that love could be found only in sex.

I was very saddened by her story, and the Lord allowed me to share with her some of the hurts of my own past life. Then I shared with her the fact that Jesus had paid a great price on Calvary to allow us all to walk free from the condemnation of the past. But when she had gone, her words stayed with me for a long time: "I was molested as a small child." What sad words those are!

Adults vs. Children

Of course, any family that suffers such a tragedy wants to keep it quiet. The child, therefore, is forced to stand there while an adult explains just why this person did such a horrible act. They didn't really mean it, and they did it only because they're sick.

In the meantime, you have a child who is frightened, hurting, ashamed and confused, and they're being told to just forget the whole incident and not think about it again. Is that even possible?

Many adults who are involved in such tragedies go away from such a confrontation smiling, as if the child has just lost a button off of her doll. She'll get over it. All is well now. It was "no big thing." And, tragically, the person who did this despicable act is still part of the happy family and, all too often, goes on to repeat it over and over again.

The Hell of Confusion

After Amnon had finished ravishing his little sister, he hated her *"exceedingly"* and told her to get out. Now little Tamar had to go through the Hell of being confused and wandering around in a daze. She was in shock. A totally innocent child, she had just met the demon of incest and come face to face with rape. On top of that, she was now being made to feel dirty and cheap, as if she was somehow to blame for what had taken place. Despair is suddenly knocking on her door.

Rape is not the only abuse that can lead to such despair. It can come through giving yourself to someone who says they love you, only to have them reject you and tear you down once they've used you for their own gratification. Suddenly they just want to cast you aside, like some dirty garment. The torment this brings to your mind is something they probably could never imagine and probably never intended when they did this thing to you.

Rape within Marriage

Rape can even occur between a husband and wife. I've spoken with women who were afraid of their husbands because of it. It is sad to think that in the United States of America in the twenty-first century a woman can be beaten and raped by her husband, and he can get away with it—because they're legally married.

I once met a man imprisoned here in Louisiana for nearly five years for having an open container of beer sitting on the back of his boat, and yet a man can walk out of one of our courthouses scot free after raping a woman— just because she happens to be his wife. This is not right.

Put Out

Amnon ordered his servant to put Tamar outside the door and bolt the door after her. Imagine how she felt in that moment. She quickly proceeded to put ashes on her head and to tear her robe.

Tearing the garment and placing ashes on the head were common acts of mourning throughout the Bible, but in this case, they seem to have had special significance. The robe Tamar tore was one that was worn only by virgins. It was scarlet in color. Now there was a scarlet stain over her life.

Usually, when ashes were placed on the head, they were symbolic, but in this case they seem to have been real hot ashes that burned the hair off and burned the skin on the head. This was a very painful experience, and apparently was one of the few ways Tamar could express the pain, the despair and the remorse that she felt. Putting ashes on your head was usually done with the death of a loved one, and I assure you that rape and molestation bring death.

At this point, Tamar then laid her hands on her head and went away shrieking and wailing. For the rest of her life, she would live as a desolate woman in the house of her brother Absalom. I am sure that at times she just wanted to die. Suicide, attempted suicide and thoughts of suicide are very common among those who find themselves the victims of rape and incest.

> *Tearing the garment and placing ashes on the head were common acts of mourning throughout the Bible!*

I Know This Pain

I know the pain of being molested by an adult I had trusted. I was molested by several different adult males before the age of six, and the experience left my life damaged. The insecurity, the distrust, the bitterness and the unforgiveness I felt as a result of it often left me crippled in a way I didn't fully understand.

And yet it often seems that the person (or persons) who have done these terrible deeds don't feel the same pain or shame and cannot understand what you're going through. You find yourself all alone, locked into a chain of consuming hate and confusion that is eating you up on the inside. You go through life wondering why your memories are all bad, why you do some of the things you do and why you make so many bad decisions in life.

Then, you go from relationship to relationship, trying to find love, without knowing in reality what love is all about. Surely love can't be the thing that caused so much pain in your life. Some run the other way, not ever wanting to touch a man again, and there are never enough baths to make them feel clean again.

I've spoken to a number of women who, after they were molested, turned to other women for comfort and their search ended badly—in lesbian sex. This even happens between mothers and daughters. I prayed with one mother and with her young girl—a victim of incest by her mother. By the grace of God, that girl's life has now turned around. She's in love with a good man, they're about to be married and she's looking forward to being a mother.

Let me add here that little girls are not the only ones to suffer rape and incest. Boys also suffer their share. And fathers are not the only ones guilty of rape and incest. Mothers also commit this sin in the perverted world in which we live.

And Satan doesn't stop with incest and rape. He sets the trap of the homosexual life-style for as many as he possibly can.

Years of Torment

For the next two years Tamar had to see the man who had caused her to lose her mind. He was laughing and going about his life as if nothing had happened, but the time of judgment would soon come for Amnon. There is always a day of reckoning with God, and the price Amnon would pay for what he had done was his life.

Tamar's story is short, but not her pain or her shame. Today hospitals are filled with women and children who have been raped and molested, and our morgues are filled with those who have been murdered by abusive relatives or have taken their own lives after being left to face the torment of what someone did to them.

I don't think anyone can know the number of unreported rapes that occur in our country every year or how many marriages end because a husband blames his wife for what happened to her. In this way, she is made to take on guilt and shame that are not rightfully hers to bear. She is made to feel that she didn't fight hard enough or that she should have killed herself rather than yield to someone's abuse.

And then there's the way Satan still lingers in the bedroom. When the husband takes his wife into his arms, all she can see is the face of the person who defiled her.

She can't help but pull away in fear and the tormenting agony of reliving that event or events all over again. Once again the enemy is at work to bring more pain into that life, and what he is doing will cause the rest of the family to suffer too. He won't be satisfied until the marriage is destroyed.

Where Do Children Turn?

> *Satan won't be satisfied until the marriage is destroyed!*

How many children have gone to their mother to report that they're being molested by a father, stepfather, boyfriend, uncle or some other family member, only to find that their own mother can't believe them? Instead of comforting them and helping them, she rebukes them and chastises them for telling such terrible lies. In this way, the little child is left alone and has no one to turn to to keep them safe.

They desperately try to blot these events out of their minds, but the scars and pain of it are still too fresh, too near the surface. And so fear continues to tear at their heart until the results are often tragic indeed.

I was blessed because I had someone to run to, my sister who was two and half years older than me. I could run to her, and she would hide me under the covers in her bed and dry my tears and help to calm my fears.

Later, looking back on it, I realized that she herself had had no one to run to, no one to hide her, to dry her tears and to make her feel safe.

Some Ministries Are Raped

Some ministries are raped, as the enemy uses evil people to destroy a work that has been ordained by God. You place your trust in certain people, and they betray you. They tell lies about you and tear down your name, leaving you little to stand on. People you have loved and supported are suddenly so full of contempt and jealousy that your dream and vision are left on the ground in pieces.

If the Shoe Fits ...

If Tamar's slipper fits your foot today, know that Jesus can restore the years the locust and the cankerworm have eaten away. He can take away your nightmares and give you a vision and a dream for a beautiful tomorrow.

Amen!

Chapter 6

Esther's Slipper

When her father and her mother died, Mordecai took
her as his own daughter.   Esther 2:7, NAS

The story of Esther is as much like a Cinderella story
as any in the Bible. Esther, beautiful Esther ... the perfect
story with the perfect ending. She and her beautiful prince
lived happily ever after.

What Heartbreak Could Esther Possibly Know?

Some might wonder what heartbreak Esther could possibly have known in life? After all, she was beautiful,
bright, young, loved and favored. And let's not forget that
she married the king. We often look at someone and

draw a mental picture of what we think their life is like—without really knowing the facts involved.

The happy ending is what God has in store for all of us, but we will have to face some trials in the meantime—and Esther did too. With this in mind, let's take a hard look at Esther's life, and in the process, let's allow the Holy Spirit to bring to light some of the hidden pain in our lives, so that we can be healed.

The Great Feast

In his third year as king, Ahasuerus of Persia threw a great party, a lavish seven-day feast. At a certain point in the feast, he ordered his queen, Vashti, to be brought in. He was proud of her and wanted to show her off to his lords. Because of this, he was extremely disappointed and angry when word came that Vashti refused to attend the feast.

This was serious. If his wife could be allowed to disobey his orders, then others might be tempted to disobey them too. In all the empire, the king's orders were law, and they could not be disobeyed. Everyone knew this. How else could he survive and rule?

When Vashti still refused to come out, the king ordered her to be made an example of. Usually the disobedient and slow to obey were immediately executed. Since she was a woman and a beautiful one at that, and since she was his wife, he ordered her to be banished from the kingdom instead. Later, the king thought of her and missed her.

Isn't That Just Like Satan?

Isn't that just like Satan? When God has brought us out of a bad relationship, the enemy will use loneliness to pull us back into it. Sometimes he uses finances. I've seen it happen many times. Women go back into ungodly relationships because they're tired of being lonely, tired of struggling to pay the bills on their own and tired of having no one to help them raise their children.

A Christian friend confided to me that he and his lady friend wanted to get married because they were both tired of being alone and single. I thought to myself, "Whatever happened to love?" I voiced some concern, but not much, because I could see that their minds were made up.

I wasn't invited to the wedding, but I saw them just a few weeks later, and she was already telling me how hard their life together was. And they were both Christians.

Today, it seems, no one is seeking God about relation-

> *When God has brought us out of a bad relationship, the enemy will use loneliness to pull us back into it!*

ships. They're just desperate to end their singleness, but they're totally unaware of and unprepared for the battles ahead that will require great love and commitment on their part. A person who is steadfast in the Lord must look beyond the flesh and into the Spirit for divine direction about marriage.

Recent statistics indicate that the divorce rate among professing Christians here in America is 52%, while among the unbelievers it's only 50%. How did that happen? And we call ourselves children of God! How foolish we sometimes act!

I'm not just pointing the finger at others. I've also been guilty of acting foolishly in this regard. It's time for us, as believers, to take off our Pampers and put on our girdle of truth before walking down the isle. Remember, we're not just playing dress-up anymore. Marriage is for real.

Some of you stood and stood, but your mate wanted out, so it's not your fault that the marriage ended. But I've had people say to me, "If it doesn't work out, we can always get a divorce." That's not a Christian attitude, and nothing is over until God says it's over. Marriage is of the utmost importance to Him. Didn't our Lord call Himself the Bridegroom? And are we not His Bride?

The Search for a Suitable Queen

This whole affair left the king very saddened, and so it was determined that another queen would be sought, one who would love and honor this man as he deserved. And the search was on among the most beautiful virgins of the Empire.

There was a Jew living in the capital whose name was Mordecai. He was a good man who had adopted and raised his uncle's daughter (his own cousin), for both of her parents were dead. Her Jewish name was Hadassah, but her Persian name was Esther. Mordecai loved her and treated her like his own daughter, and I'm sure that she loved and respected him like a father in return.

Esther was spoken of as being both beautiful and lovely, and I've taken this to mean that she was a very gentle person. When it became known throughout the kingdom that a new queen was being sought, Mordecai immediately thought of Esther and encouraged her to join the competition. That alone speaks very highly of her.

But can you imagine how this all must have seemed to Esther at the time? She was about to face life-changing circumstances, one way or another.

I can imagine Esther's heart racing with the thought of it: not only of possibly being chosen as queen, but also of being separated from the only family she knew. Mordecai was all that she had left in this world, the only person she felt safe with, and if she accepted this challenge she must now go to live in the palace among strangers. Although she trusted her cousin, she must have felt very confused at that moment, and she must have felt a certain amount of fear. For sure, she had to be full of questions. To any young lady, having to leave the family for the first time is a traumatic experience.

Maybe you can relate to Esther's experience. I know I can. Because of death, separation, divorce or even sickness, disability or poverty, children are sometimes shunted from one relative to another. At times, it's even necessary for the State to step in and remove a child from the home for their own safety when their parents are considered unfit. What a tragedy this is!

> *Because of death, separation, divorce or even sickness, disability or poverty, children are sometimes shunted from one relative to another!*

I Remember the Day Well

I remember the day well—although many years have passed since then. The sun was shining brightly, and it seemed to be around midday when some strange people came to the door and said they were from the State, and they were going to have to put me into Foster Care, because my mother was staying away from home so much.

Sometimes she would go out, saying that she was going to the store or to visit our father in the VA hospital, but then she didn't come back for days at a time. Alone at home, I would sometimes get a phone call in the early morning hours, asking me to come and get my mother because she was too drunk to drive, or if Dad was home, he would sometimes ask me to go find her, and I would have to go and bring her back home. I was only twelve, and, of course, I didn't have a driver's license, but there was no one else to do it. Diane had married young and now had her own life, and Dutch had run away from home.

I couldn't much blame him. Seeing our parents drunk had become a way of life for all three of us, and we had to learn to survive by our own wits. Once, when we were younger, the three of us had gone with Dad to pick Mom up, and he passed out on the way. Somehow we were able to pull him over to the passenger's side of the car, and then Diane steered the car, while Dutch sat on the floorboard and pushed the gas and brake peddles when she told him it was needed. I think they were around ten, and I was about eight at the time. I know the Lord had to have been with us. Now, about four years later, Mom wasn't home again, Dad was back in the hospital (he spent years there), and these strangers were standing at the door saying that they had to take me away.

It Was the Only Home I Knew

Our home wasn't much of a home, but it was the only home I knew. I stood there pleading with them not to take me away from it. "Let me call my mom on the phone," I urged. I knew all the bars where she hung out, and I was sure that I could find her. I knew she wouldn't let them take me away. She loved me too much for that.

I wasn't a bad girl. I made sure I was always home before dark. I came straight home from school. And I never talked back. Even if Mom wasn't at home, I stayed there, waiting for her to come home or to call me to come get her. Surely she would stop them from taking me now. They agreed to let me call.

I called the club where I was sure Mom was and told her what was happening. These people wanted to take me away. Could she please come home and stop them. Her answer was not what I had expected at all. "No," she said, "I have my own life to live." And she hung up.

What Was Happening?

I stood there for the longest time trying to understand what was happening. Satan was working overtime to destroy both her and me. Only twelve, I was suddenly more alone than ever and very frightened. Added to what I had already experienced, now were the new pains of rejection, the strong desire to be loved and the need for a home I could call my own. These were scars that would last a lifetime—if not dealt with.

Many people think they've successfully hidden the scars of their past, but there is still a trail of blood that affects them every single day. Far too many of us are still hurting from the events of our yesterdays.

Probably the saddest part of this equation is that we victims carry the aftermath of our childhood abuse into the lives of our own children. And, to some degree, we then become just like our abusers. For, to us, that's the only normal we know.

Insisting

The State workers kept insisting that we had to go, and I kept insisting that they couldn't take me, that we had to find some other solution. I couldn't bear the thought of losing my home. Eventually they allowed me to call Diane, and she and her husband came over right away to speak with them and help me argue my cause. It was finally agreed that if Diane's husband would take full responsibility for me, I could be released into their custody to go and live with them. This was better than being sent to a foster home, but I still had to leave the home I loved. It was so sad gathering up my few belongings and taking them away from that place.

Sometimes Mom would come to visit Diane's, and each time, before she left, I would beg her to let me go home with her. I remember running alongside her car, calling out to her, pleading with her to take me, and she wouldn't. This only increased my feelings of rejection and disappointment.

The story, however, has a more happy ending. After I

had lived with Diane and her husband for several months, Mom relented and let me move back home. Nothing much else had changed, but at least I wasn't stranded among strangers.

By God's grace, in later years, major healing occurred in my life and also in my mother's life. We both gave our lives to Jesus, and before she departed this world, we had many good years of loving each other. She'd had her own Hell to deal with, and I'd had mine, but Jesus held the keys, and, thank God, He set us both free.

Removed from the Home

Esther was now taken to Shushan, the capital, and placed in the care of a man named Hegai. He was the Keeper of the Women. As she had pleased Mordecai, Esther now pleased Hegai and obtained favor with him.

Some of you know what it is to be placed in the care of others. In some cases, it's for the best, but unfortunately it's not always so. Some foster homes are wonderful, and the children who go there are blessed to have a happy ending to their situation. Some are eventually restored to their normal home life, and some are adopted. But there are others who are beaten, starved and molested. This is not true only of small children, and it is equally true of boys as it is of girls.

Even grown women who become victims of divorce, abuse, sickness or the death of a spouse often find themselves in places they don't want to be. They've had no choice in the matter. In those moments, they are full of questions and have many fears they don't understand and cannot express. They experience the trauma of rejection and abandonment.

What spirit has torn your heart apart? Is it the feeling of not belonging? Has someone made you feel that you owed them something for a place to lay your head or the small morsel of bread they provided? Maybe you have been shunted around from aunt to aunt or cousin to cousin, or just had to survive alone on your own. Jesus has never left me, and He has never left you.

Just the Opposite?

Maybe it was just the opposite. Maybe you were a parent who left a child, and you have repented for it over and over, time and time again, and yet Satan continues to keep you oppressed and depressed over what you did. He tells you what a worthless parent you are

> *She'd had her own Hell to deal with, and I'd had mine, but Jesus held the keys, and, thank God, He set us both free!*

and were, and so now you spend year after year trying to make up for the wrongs you did in the past. But no matter how hard you try, your children just can't seem to forgive you, or you can't seem to forgive yourself.

Jesus forgave you the moment you asked Him to and took your life in a different direction. He can give you wisdom and strength to bring your children home, to undo the work Satan has done in an attempt to destroy your childhood and/or your children's childhood. We can't undo the past, but with Jesus, we can build a wonderful future that will produce healing from the past.

Remember, Esther went on to marry the king. God gave her a wonderful future that would bring much joy and laughter. And let's not forget love.

If the Shoe Fits ...

If Esther's slipper fits your foot and you still have scars from being alone as a child—insecure, unwanted and unloved—allow Jesus to place a slipper of love and healing upon your heart, soul, mind and spirit. He loves you so much that He spread His arms wide and died for you.

Amen!

Chapter 7

Ruth's Slipper

Then she said, "Behold, your sister-in-law has gone back to her people and her gods; return after your sister-in-law."

But Ruth said, "Do not urge me to leave you or turn back from following you; for where you go, I will go, and where you lodge, I will lodge. Your people shall be my people, and your God, my God. Where you die, I will die, and there I will be buried. Thus may the LORD do to me, and worse, if anything but death parts you and me." Ruth 1:15-17, NAS

Sometimes, as we look through the pages of someone else's life, we're somehow able see ourselves more clearly. By looking closely at what they suffered and how they

> **Like most of us, Ruth experienced both pain and laughter, sorrow and joy, but then she was suddenly hit with the uncertainty of her future!**

reacted to it, we become enlightened about things we never knew or understood before.

Faced with Uncertainty

Ruth's life was pretty hard for a while, I think. It surely wasn't any bed of roses. Like most of us, she experienced both pain and laughter, sorrow and joy. But then she was suddenly hit with the uncertainty of her future. Many calamites, working together, seemed to overtake her life, and she was faced with great despair. It is in such moments that we discover what is really in our hearts, and all too often, we find it to be empty. But Ruth's time of despair was turned around, and yours can be too.

There is much pain to be seen in the book of Ruth, but we can leave all pain behind, for the Scriptures declare:

Weeping may endure for a night, but joy cometh in the morning.
Psalm 30:5

"Joy cometh in the morning," and, Honey, it is almost daylight.

Married to an Invalid

Ruth was married to a man named Mahlon, which means "invalid." If he was anything like his name, he wasn't a very healthy person. It's quite possible that Mahlon required a lot of care.

Ruth was a giving person, and the story shows this time and time again. She was dedicated, committed and very loving. Strong, yet very gentle ... that's how I see her. She was no stranger to pain, and that made her full of compassion for others.

Ruth had a sister named Orpah. They were women of Moab, and they married brothers from Bethlehem, men who were living in Moab at the time with their mother Naomi. Their father had died, and now they were their mother's sole support.

Ruth was still a young woman, but only ten years into her marriage to Mahlon, he too died. Then, in short order, his brother, the husband of Orpah, also died. Ruth had left her family and all that she knew to marry a man of a different culture and different religion, and now he was dead, and her world was suddenly turned upside down.

She couldn't go to her sister for comfort, for Orpah had her own pain to deal with. She also couldn't go to her mother-in-law for comfort. Naomi had lost her husband, and now she had lost both of her sons.

The circumstances of life sometimes seem to pile on us to make our plight worse, until life itself seems to be little more than one gigantic heartache. No wonder people sometimes ask, "Why me? Am I such a terrible person? Will there ever be such a thing as happiness for me again?"

Divorce Is Like Death

It is often said that divorce is, in many ways, like death. Something or someone has died. Your hope, your joy, your laughter and your expectations are all gone in the blink of an eye. All the dreams of a wonderful future have somehow slipped through your fingers like grains of sand and are gone. I don't think anyone is ready for the death of a loved one or for the death of a marriage.

I know I wasn't, and I grieved over it for years, feeling all the pain, all the emotions of someone who had been to Hell and back. There was so much hurt that the least little thing could bring it all back to the surface again.

When people paired off at family functions to take photos, I slowly died all over again. I could never go to family gatherings without this happening, and the holidays were always the worst. When it came to the holidays, I just wanted to run and hide to escape the pain. I couldn't see that this was hurting the rest of the family because I was so lost in my own agony. And no one else could understand what I was feeling or why.

"Whither Thou Goest, I Will Go"

It seems that Ruth loved her mother-in-law deeply. Although the Bible doesn't say much about her personal pain, it does say that she wept at the thought of being separated from Naomi.

For her part, Naomi was nearly beyond consolation. If she had not known the Lord, the pain of recent events would have destroyed her, and Ruth probably would have been destroyed with her. I can see God's grace upon the two of them, and that grace has been and still is with you and with me today.

After the death of her husband and her sons, Naomi tried to get Ruth and Orpah to go back to their own people. She now had no way of supporting them. She couldn't even support herself. Orpah agreed, but Ruth wouldn't go. She insisted that she would go where Naomi went, and live where Naomi lived. Naomi's people would now become her people, and Naomi's God would be her God. She would die where Naomi died and be buried where Naomi was buried. Nothing but death would separate them.

This shows that Ruth's heart was still very tender, not full of bitterness at all. She was determined to go with Naomi back to Bethlehem, for she was determined to continue worshiping Naomi's God. She was convinced that He was the miracle-working God. And, wonder of wonders, one day God's Son, Jesus Christ, would be born to the very descendents of this same Ruth, the Moabitess.

Returning to Bethlehem

When Ruth and Naomi arrived at Bethlehem, the people were happy to see them and said, "Is this Naomi" (meaning pleasant)?

Naomi answered them, "Call me Mara" (meaning bitter), "for God has dealt with me bitterly." What sad words!

Some of you, too, know the bitterness of the death of a spouse or the death of a marriage due to divorce. No matter how the separation comes, a marriage has ended. Something has died, and Satan will do his best to bring you bitterness because of it.

Again, Ruth did not appear to be bitter, and I have sometimes wondered about that. Was she not angry at all, on top of the hurt she had to be feeling and the fact that she surely must have been frightened at what the future held for her and Naomi? What an extraordinary lady!

Suddenly Alone and Abandoned

I knew a lady who had a wonderful husband, a man who took very good care of her. They were both still in their forties. She got cancer, but he was in good health. Then one day, out of the blue, he suddenly and unexpectedly died.

She was in disbelief at first. Next, she went into a phase in which she was deeply hurt. And finally, she became very angry. How could he just leave her like that when she needed him the most? She was sick, broke and alone and with so much pain. What could she do now? How would she make it in life? What was he thinking?

Many women experience this same pain with divorce, and those very same questions torment their minds. "How could he leave me like this, all alone, hurting and dying inside, with nowhere to turn and no place to escape to?"

> *Many women experience this same pain with divorce, and those very same questions torment their minds!*

It May Have Been Your Child

It may have been your child who left you to live with the other parent after the divorce. Think of it. That child has gone to live with the very person who has caused all your dreams to fall to the ground. Why on earth would any child want to leave *you* and go with *him*?

Now you're even more confused and hurt, and you wonder how to turn your heart off and stop feeling. It's not safe even to love your own children.

I know what that feels like, for I experienced all of this pain and believed all the lies Satan told me because of it. I suddenly didn't know how to show love to anyone anymore. All I knew to do was run as fast as I could, thinking that maybe I would wake up and this terrible nightmare would be over, and I would have my family back.

The sad part is that I ran so far away from my children that, for a while, I couldn't seem to find my way back into their hearts in the way a mother should. It was only by the grace of God that I eventually began to feel loved and wanted by them again, and they began to feel loved and wanted by me.

There Is Hope

There is always hope. How do I know? Because Jesus said it, and I believe it. If you have lost someone to death, and you feel all of these mixed emotions, know that your loved one didn't want to leave you. They didn't have a choice in the matter. It was just their appointed time. They didn't intend to leave you behind, hurting and having to face life all alone. But they are aware of the fact that Jesus will help you make it through until you meet them again.

What do I mean by this? I believe that your loved ones are in Heaven even now, praying for you, while you're still here on earth. I can say this with assurance because Jesus took me to Heaven in 1989, and one of the things I saw was dramatically etched upon my memory. There were people as far as I could see, and they were all on their knees, praying for their loved ones still on earth. So if you have lost a child, sister, brother, father, mother, husband or anyone else dear to you, know that Heaven is real, that they're happy there, and that you'll see them again someday.

Maybe you're even bitter toward God. Many are. But think about it this way: Death is a reward God gives His children, not some punishment meant to torment you. God knew that you would hurt when you lost a loved one, and He loves you. But He also loved the person who died, and He loved them enough to take them home to be free of the pain of this world. The Word of God teaches us:

We are confident, I say, and willing rather to be absent from the body, and to be present with the Lord.
2 Corinthians 5:8

That settles it.

My Brother Dutch Was a Modern-day Good Samaritan

Even though we know that our loved ones are with the Lord, we still can't help but ask why? I was faced with this question more than once. The last time was when my brother Dutch died.

If there ever was a Good Samaritan, Dutch was one. He didn't have much of this world's goods, due to his poor health, and yet he was full of love for everyone he met. He would pick up hitchhikers and then take them to his home and feed them. He even let them take a bath in his bathroom and then urged them to get a good night's sleep in one of his beds before putting them back on the road the next day.

If Dutch had the money, he would even pay their bus fare home. Many times he would borrow money to help feed someone he had met on the road. He had so much love to give, that it's difficult to understand why he was given so little of life's goods.

> *Some people die before their time because of unwise decisions!*

But then his life was cut short. Three weeks after Dutch received Jesus as his Lord and Savior, he died, crushed to death beneath a mobile home. Jesus knew that we would hurt because of this loss, and He hurt with us.

Why Some Die Prematurely

Some people die before their time because of unwise decisions. I warned Dutch not to get under that trailer. The ground was too wet, and I was sure that someone was going to get hurt. But he wouldn't listen, and so he died. Because he didn't use wisdom, his life was cut short.

People make decisions every day that cause them to experience an early death, but we should never believe that everyone who dies before their time has done something unwise. With some, an early death is God's mercy.

He has taken them home to be with Him. His Word tells us:

The righteous perisheth, and no man layeth it to heart: and merciful men are taken away, none considering that the righteous is taken away from the evil to come.
Isaiah 57:1

Sometimes Satan's plan is so bad for us that Jesus steps in and says to him, "Oh, no you don't! I'll show you! I'll take him (or her) home to be with Me, and then you can't touch them." What seems to us like an untimely death is really God's mercy at work.

When anyone we love dies, it's never God's plan to hurt us, and He never wants those of us who are left behind to be full of regrets—our "should'ves," "would'ves" and "could'ves." Regrets can eat you alive, and so can the guilt of not having been there, of not having said, "I love you" more, and of not having spent more time with that person, now lying lifeless in a casket.

My brother got up from the table, after having eaten lunch, and five minutes later he was dead. When I got that news, it was too late to spend time with him, as he had been trying to get me to do. For more than three years after that, I lived with the Hell of that regret.

I suffered terrible feelings of guilt for another reason. Just before the trailer fell, I had a vision of it. So I had seen it and knew that it was going to happen, and yet I didn't pick up the phone to call my brother and warn him about it again. I knew it would happen, and yet I didn't follow through to understand what to do to prevent it. So I spent the next three years thinking that if I had just called Dutch and told him what I had seen, he would still be alive and helping people like he loved to do.

But we can never undo the past, so we have to go on. The truth is that maybe it was Dutch's time to go, and maybe he wouldn't have answered the telephone. Who knows? But the enemy used those thoughts to torment my mind. It was only after three years of immeasurable suffering that I was able to allow Jesus to take away that horrible guilt and to bring healing to my heart.

Maybe Satan has tormented you in this same way, with guilt that is not rightfully yours to bear. But just as Jesus took all my guilt away and brought me healing, He can do the same for you.

It wasn't your fault, so let it go, and let Jesus send His healing waters over your tormented mind and soul. Now let's get back to Ruth.

Ruth Had Purposed in Her Heart

Ruth had purposed in her heart to care for her mother-in-law. Therefore she put aside her own pain and her own needs, to meet the needs of a woman who seemed to have little or no hope. Ruth was willing to give of herself and to put others first. Their needs must come before her own.

Maybe you have done this same thing, putting others

before yourself, doing without so that someone else didn't have to do without. If that's the case, then, Honey, it's harvest time. With Jesus, you're just a miracle in the making. The Lord tells us:

And let us not be weary in well-doing: for in due season we shall reap, if we faint not.   Galatians 6:9

God had a plan for both Ruth and Naomi, and it was a wonderful plan.

Boaz Comes on the Scene

Naomi had a relative, a man of wealth, whose name was Boaz. He was soon to come upon the scene.

Still caring for her mother-in-law, Ruth went into the field daily to glean what little grain she could find left behind by the harvesters. She worked hard, put food on the table and remained dedicated to Naomi's welfare. And this did not go unnoticed.

When Ruth was seen in his field one day, Boaz asked the reapers who this young women was. They told him of Ruth and Naomi, and in this way, he learned that these women were, in fact, relatives of his. When he next saw Ruth, he told her not to worry about going into other fields. She should stay in his fields and expect to reap enough for their needs.

That was like Jesus telling us, His daughters, to stay close to Him and to the ministry He has called us to. His desire is to send us out into the field of broken hearts, not only to give hope to others, but also to find hope for ourselves once again. We can glean behind the reapers, and our own needs will be supplied.

This new development was encouraging to Ruth and Naomi. Even after death, life does go on. Whether it is the death of a spouse or the death of a marriage, it doesn't have to be the end of your life or of your joy. God has something good in store for you.

Break All Soul-Ties

Of course, remarriage is what most women desire, and Ruth was surely ready for that too. Her heart was set toward the future, not the past, and yet perhaps she needed some time to seek the Lord for complete healing of all her wounds.

There's something else to consider, something most people overlook. One of the most damaging tools Satan uses to hinder relationships is to cause us to have a soul-tie to someone else from the past. If you're unable or unwilling to let go of the soul-ties of the past, any new marriage will suffer.

You don't have to be married to someone to have a soul-tie with them. Everyone has a soul-tie to someone. And such a soul-tie can keep you from surrendering your whole heart to a new mate, even one ordained by God Himself.

If you are holding hands with someone you're about

to marry, or you're in the arms of someone you have recently married, and your thoughts go to someone you knew before, that's devastating to any relationship.

If you're remembering, desiring or longing to be with someone else other than your current mate, that's not good. It's not good for your new relationship, and it's not good for your relationship with God. And, if you keep it up, you'll dig such a deep hole of discontent that you won't be able to get out of it. Honey, you're not only cheating yourself out of a fulfilling relationship; you're cheating your husband, and you're robbing God of the glory due Him for having put this person into your life.

The Third Person

Maybe you're in a relationship, and you can't help but feel that there is often a third person with you in the room. What's worse, they may be with you in the bed. (And when I refer to a

> *One of the most damaging tools Satan uses to hinder relationships is to cause us to have a soul-tie to someone else from the past!*

third person in the relationship, I'm certainly not talking about Jesus).

You feel that your man loves you, and yet you sense that he's actually thinking of someone else, someone from his past. That tears at your heart, because you want to be the only woman in his thoughts and dreams. And he wants to be the only one in yours too.

What's interfering in this marriage is a spirit called a soul-tie, and it keeps a person from letting go and yielding themselves to another. Jesus can set you free from this, if you will ask Him to. Then you can find true love again.

Healing is a big part of starting over, but we can never walk in a new beginning until we have let go of the past— all of it. We can't change life, but Jesus died so that we could have life and have it *"more abundantly."*

Ruth Married Boaz

In time, Ruth went on to marry Boaz, and Naomi was full of joy at the birth of their son. She began to live again. You and I need to stop asking for what we had in the past and start believing, like Job, for a better future. His past had been glorious, but now it was all gone. Still, rather then grieve for what was, he believed God for something better, and he received seven times more than he'd had before.

This it the time for restoration in the lives of God's people. Let it happen, not only in your own life, but also in the lives of your children, your parents and your ministry.

If the Shoe Fits ...

So if Ruth's slipper fits your foot today, allow Jesus to break the old soul-ties and place the slipper of deliverance, healing, hope and the joy of a new beginning onto your foot of a restored life.

Amen!

Chapter 8

The Woman with
the Issue of Blood's Slipper

*And a woman who had a hemorrhage for twelve years,
and could not be healed by anyone, came up behind
Him and touched the fringe of His cloak, and immediately her hemorrhage stopped.* Luke 8:43-44, NAS

As we travel on into the New Testament, where we
see Jesus at work, we want to stop and ponder about a
character we meet in the book of Luke. She was a woman
suffering from long-term internal hemorrhaging. For a
moment, let's stand with many others in a crowd, watching, as Jesus comes down the street.

There are so many people, and they're pressed so
tightly around Jesus that I don't know why He's not suf-
focated. People are pushing and shoving, reaching out to

touch this Man, for they have either heard of His power to heal and forgive, or they've seen Him do it before. It is said that He even raises dead people, cleanses lepers and makes the blind to see and the lame to walk. It seems that there is nothing this great Man, this Messiah, cannot do. It's no wonder, then, that people are pushing for an opportunity to ask Him to pray for *them* and to heal *them*.

She Couldn't Reach Him

With all this crowd around Jesus, the woman with the issue of blood couldn't reach Him, as much as she tried. Then, as He passed nearer, she made one last heroic effort, reaching out as far as she possibly could, and she was able to touch just the hem, or fringe, of His garment. But that was enough. In that moment, Jesus suddenly stopped and asked, "Who touched Me?"

Peter and the rest of those who were with Jesus just looked at Him and said, "What do You mean, who touched You? Can You not see the people pressing against You from every side?"

Jesus answered them, "I felt power flowing out of Me."

Isn't that just like Jesus? When we call on Him, with a prayer from our hearts, He knows our voice and our touch, just as we, His children, know His voice and, yes, His touch as well. Isn't it wonderful to know that we serve a God who, even when we're in a crowd, knows when we need to feel His touch or to hear His voice?

Jesus not only hears our cry; He instantly stops to listen. And He not only listens; He then helps us to move into a holy place of prayer with a pure heart and to get in tune with His miraculous healing power. The result is that it flows straight into us. Oh, my friends, with just a whisper, we can touch the hem of His garment.

We Don't Know Her Name

The Bible doesn't tell this woman's name, but it lets us know the serious issue she was facing in life. She had been hemorrhaging for a very long time, and therefore, her health was put at serious risk. In an effort to try to get well, she had spent all of her money, her time and her strength on the known remedies of the day, and still she got worse. Twelve years is a long time to go to doctors and not get any better!

Maybe you have issues in your

> *When we call on Him, ... He knows our voice and our touch, just as we, His children, know His voice and His touch!*

life. You have poured out all of your heart, and yet you're sick—in your body, your heart, your soul, your mind and maybe even your spirit. It is sad to say that just as we can become physically sick, we can also become spiritually sick.

"How is that?" someone might ask. In some cases our sickness comes through bitterness and unforgiveness. We can either drink from the sweet waters of forgiveness and maintain a tender heart, or we can drink from bitter waters and become hardened in our hearts. Unforgiveness and bitterness are not only held toward other men and women, but also toward God.

Are we ready to be honest with ourselves and with God and to lay down the self-righteous mask the enemy wants us to hide behind? It is a mask that says, "I've never been upset with God." If we will lay it down, then we can touch the hem of Jesus' garment and receive the healing He died for us to have.

Why, God?

I don't know how to make this any plainer. I had to learn this truth, just as I'm sharing it with you now through the pages of this book. I had to come to a place that I was honest enough to admit that I had questions for God. I was asking Him how He could have allowed me to be so terribly hurt. Why did He allow a person to hurt me in such a way?

Please don't misunderstand me. I had put all my faith and trust in God, and He was my God, but now I was questioning Him. In the end, I came to understand that He had not failed me. As I allowed the river of His life to fill my belly with sweet, vibrant waters, I was healed— physically, emotionally and spiritually.

Many people I have counseled with have had this same problem. Because their relationship with their man began to fall apart or ended altogether, they began questioning God: How could He have allowed this to happen? They were sure that He had guided them to this very mate, and now they had lost him? "Why, God?" they pray.

So now they have two issues to deal with. They had an issue with the person who hurt them, and now they also have an issue with God. The result is distrust and a lack of belief in His Word. I've heard some go so far as to say, "Why did I refrain from sex, not even dating, just waiting for the right man to come along, the one God would send? I could have married a nonbeliever and been better off than I am now."

Satan Is Crafty

You don't have to look very deep to see the pain such a person feels. But look a little closer, and you'll see something else, something very dangerous indeed. Bitterness is attempting to take root in them, and it is a bitterness against God Himself. Just like me, this person now finds it hard to pray, and the joy they once had in reading His Word has faded. Now, instead of joyful, they often find themselves angry.

Satan is crafty at what he tells you. He is so crafty that you may not even realize that it's the Lord you have an issue with. The enemy wants you to remain ignorant of this fact. He loves it when you stop praying and stop reading the Word.

I've heard people say, "But God owes me." Honey, He doesn't owe you or me a thing.

I heard one lady say, "I pay my tithes, so God owes me." It's true that if we keep His command-ments, statues and judgments, we are entitled to receive His prom-ises. But, although I can't speak for you, I can say that I'm not perfect yet (even though I strive for it). I still have to depend on His mercy and compassion that is renewed every morning. It is because of what Jesus did at Calvary that I can walk in His righteousness.

It all comes down to the fact that Jesus loves us. His love is ev-erlasting, never-ending. As the apostle Paul wrote:

> *I've heard others pray, "Bring him back, Lord!" But then they add something to their prayer: "But change him first!"*

For I am persuaded beyond doubt (am sure) that nei-ther death nor life, nor angels nor principalities, nor

things impending and threatening nor things to come,
nor powers, nor height nor depth, nor anything else in
all creation will be able to separate us from the love of
God which is in Christ Jesus our Lord.

Romans 8:38-39, AMP

Jesus loves you so much that even in that midnight hour, when all you can do is reprove Him because of your pain, He is still holding you. You don't even realize that you're doing it, but you are. You're actually cursing God and saying in essence that He has done something bad to cause you pain. But the one and only true God loves you intensely.

Our Confusing Prayers

Some have prayed, "Get me out of this marriage, Lord. I can't take it anymore." Then, when they're delivered, they cry out, "Why, Lord? Why are we not together anymore? Bring him back to me." What's God to do? Such prayers are confusing to anyone.

I've heard others pray, "Bring him back, Lord!" But then they add something to their prayer: "But change him first." And then they add something else: "And if he's not going to change, then don't bring him back at all." But then, when the man doesn't change and he doesn't come back, God gets all the blame. It's time that we get rid of the confusion, decide what we want from God and start obeying His Word.

Nothing Left but Her Faith

This woman now had nothing left but faith, but she did have that, and faith in God can make you whole. When any of us are told by a doctor that we have a disease that's incurable and that there is no medical help for us, it's no reason to become angry with God. Our tendency is to become bitter and resentful and to ask Him questions like:

"Why me, God?"
"Where are You when I need You?"
"What did I do wrong?"

Before I was saved, I smoked and did drugs, and because of it, I developed emphysema and I've also suffered from asthma through the years. Then, over the past few years, I came to know that I have what is called COPD, a very serious lung disease. There are medications that help control this disease, but there is no cure, and those who suffer from COPD usually live for only seven to ten years.

So I've had to make a choice. I can either believe the promises of God's Word, or I can wallow in misery and self-pity. When I first received this diagnosis, I was pleased to find that I was not blaming God and neither was I questioning His love for me. I've come to know who He is and what He's like. His Word promises:

If you diligently heed the voice of the LORD your God and do what is right in His sight, give ear to His commandments and keep all His statutes, I will put none of the diseases on you which I have brought on the Egyptians. For I am the LORD who heals you.

Exodus 15:26, NKJ

Because of His promises, I have a great peace about my health.

One day I was praying for very needy people to be healed. Some needed limbs to grow out, and others needed equally extraordinary miracles. I was praying for them, not for myself, but suddenly I looked up, and I had what is called an open vision. I saw some objects floating in the air and was totally puzzled by what I was seeing. "Lord, what is that?" I asked.

"Those are lungs," the Lord said. "I'm going to heal you. I'm going to give you lungs as pink as a newborn baby's."

To this day, I cling to that very personal promise of healing. I do not believe that we must die to be healed. Among believers, some are healed and some are not, but I know what God promised me, and I have no doubt that it will come to pass.

I have peace about my situation, and I refuse to blame God, because He is my hope.

I refuse to believe the lies of the enemy. Rather, I have chosen to trust God, and I know that my reward will come.

You, too, can trust the promises of God's Word, for He never lies:

God is not a man, that he should lie.
He is not a human, that he should change his mind.
Has he ever spoken and failed to act?
Has he ever promised and not carried it through?

Numbers 23:19, NLT

God is faithful. He's always been there for me, and I know He always will be. There is no doubt in my mind that if He could heal this desperate woman in the Bible and He could heal me, He can also heal you today.

Desperate

The woman was desperate, and she was convinced that if she could just touch the hem of Jesus' garment, she would be healed. But that wasn't an easy thing to do. Yes, she was desperate, but so were many others. And everyone was trying to get close to Jesus. To reach Him took great effort on her part. She was so weakened in her body by the constant loss of blood that she didn't have the strength required to press past other, more able-bodied, people. And it didn't help that they, too, were trying to get to Jesus.

But this woman had made up her mind. She would push through. She would reach out. She would believe for her healing. So it didn't matter to her what others were doing or not doing around her. She was focused on her own need and on reaching Jesus to have it met.

And you and I need to come to that same place, the place where it no longer matters if our man comes back or if he changes. All that's important at the moment is that we be healed and set free of all bitterness, anger and unforgive-ness.

Some of us need to repent for blaming God for our pain. It wasn't His desire for you to be hurt or be-trayed. It was and still is His plan for all men and woman to walk in the fullness of the fruit of His Spirit, so that they can also walk in the fullness of His truth, His mercy and His compassion for others. If we could all do that, this kind of pain, caused by the men and women we love, would never exist.

> *You, too, can trust the promises of God's Word, for He never lies!*

If the Shoe Fits ...

If this slipper fits the foot of your life and your par-ticular issues, then allow the Holy Spirit to slip the garment of praise upon your heart so that through the Holy Spirit and the blood of Jesus you can be set free of all bitterness and unforgiveness and can pray with a pure heart. To-day, in the twenty-first century, we can still touch the hem of His garment. Let Jesus heal all those old hurts and wounds, so that you can push through to your miracle.

Amen!

Chapter 9

Mary Magdalene's Slipper

Now after He had risen early on the first day of the week, He first appeared to Mary Magdalene, from whom He had cast out seven demons.

Mark 16:9, NAS

As we near the end of our journey through the lives of some of the great women of the Bible, we now find ourselves walking along the Sea of Galilee. We come to a small village known as Magdala. It is said that a woman by the name of Mary lived there. Because of that, she was called Mary Magdalene. It was also said that Mary Magdalene was a great sinner, a prostitute, a woman of many problems—according to some writings—and certainly of many demons. This woman had many serious moral and emotional issues to face.

Not Much Is Said of Her

> *You may not have been a prostitute, like Mary, but you may be walking through life feeling just as dirty as if you were!*

There isn't much written in the Bible about Mary Magdalene, but what we do read of her warms our hearts. Jesus liked her, and I do too. In fact, she has been a favorite of many down through the ages. And, although little was written of her, what is written still has a lot to say to us in our time.

You may not have been a prostitute, like Mary, but you may be walking through life feeling just as dirty as if you were. And maybe you either are or were a prostitute. If you were one in the past, I'm sure that Satan is still using your yesterdays to destroy all of your tomorrows, not to mention your todays.

People have a tendency to label us by what they see on the outside. What they cannot see is the pain and grief we bear. Thank God that Jesus not only heals the sick; He also forgives and transforms the sinner. If selling yourself is your life, then you are surely sick in spirit. But there is good news: I know the Healer.

Running in Search of Something

You may have run from club to club or even from man to man, trying to find a way to survive in this world. If so, it's because you felt so confused, so lost and so afraid. And running seemed, in your muddled thinking, to be the only solution, the only answer.

I've known some women who were prostitutes, and usually they were doing it to try to support a drug habit or their man. Some were trying to support their children until they could find someone who would marry them and help support them. These women didn't see having sex to earn money for food as being prostitution, but of course, it is. Satan is able to deceive many, young and old alike, and he thus sends them straight into a Hell on earth, a life of constant torment.

And think about the children of these women, watching and listening through closed doors. What would make a woman take such a risk? At some point, demons have come in and are controlling her mind.

Satan respects no age or sex. Many prostitutes get their start in the trade between the ages of twelve and fourteen, and some even younger. Some of them are convinced that it's the only way they can survive. Others are runaways, who find themselves alone and stranded on the streets of our cities, easy prey for the demon-controlled men and women who lurk in wait for them. For others, prostitution is a way to get rich quick and be able to have the fine clothes, the fancy apartments and the expensive cars they so desire.

Thank God!

Thank God, I never got into prostitution myself, but it wasn't because I was so good. It had to have been God, in His mercy, who turned a light on in my head and let me know just how crazy this life-style is.

Because I didn't sleep around a lot, I considered myself to be a fairly moral person, and it therefore shocked me one day when I was approached at a club I frequented. A woman came up to me. I had seen her around the club, and I admired her. She had told me that she was an insurance salesperson, and she certainly seemed to have it all together. She drove a Mercedes and wore fine suites. "She has everything a girl could want in life," I thought ... until that day she approached me and asked if I would like to have a job. She guaranteed me a new car and a nice place to live, but as it turned out, this "insurance salesperson" was a high-priced prostitute.

It was very offensive to me that she had thought of me as someone willing to hire out my body. She had to think that or she would never have made me such a nightmare of an offer. This fact played on my mind and became a serious factor in how I began to see myself. And from that point on, things went from bad to worse for me. People label you, and Satan lays claim to you, but Jesus died for you so that you can be delivered.

Caught Up

Once a person gets caught up in the club life, it's very hard for them to break away from it. Nightclubs are dark places, full of demonic forces. There is plenty of lust, deceit, lies, betrayal, perversion, fornication, adultery, drugs and booze ... and most anything else you can name. If it's a sin, you can find it in a nightclub. To me, at first, it was just a place to dance and have a good time. I didn't even drink. But it doesn't take Satan long to blind us to what the door to Hell looks like.

Like me, most club-goers start out because of a broken heart. They're lonely. They're hurting. They're lost. And they're running from all the pain inside that they somehow can't express, and most of all, can't get rid of. They're so afraid, and they're trying to find someone who can help them put their life and their dreams back together again.

But this is a life-style that can never have good consequences. It only makes things worse, not better. Of course I couldn't see that at the time. It was part of Satan's deception. He's out to destroy you and to destroy what's left of your family.

Desiring Respect

I'm sure that Mary Magdalene, at some point, dreamed of having a family and of having the respect of the people around her. Sadly, this world is full of Pharisees, those who can only seem to judge and condemn. They can't see the torment and the pain a person is suffering.

Your Pharisees may be the members of your own family. They may be strangers. Or, worse yet, they may be "church folk." Whatever the case, the pain they cause with their ignorance is still the same.

But when we get caught up in drugs and alcohol, we quickly lose our moral bearing. Maybe *quickly* is not the right word. Sometimes the progression, or transformation, that takes place in us is so slow that we don't even realize that it's happening. Often we don't realize how much we have changed until this thing has us firmly in its ugly grip.

And some people don't seem to know any better. Drugs, alcohol and sex is all they've ever known. Their life here is a kind of Sodom and Gomorrah.

It's very possible that you have been caught up in a life-style of prostitution (even if it wasn't for money), and that life-style has left you marked. Your name is destroyed, and you are widely considered to be a nobody—dirty, unclean. Some might even use words like *whore* or *drunk* to describe you. Somehow you never saw yourself in this way, but people can be very cruel.

Our Lord Jesus is full of love, mercy and compassion. Even if your sin is *"red like crimson,"* He said, He's ready to wash you *"as white as snow"*:

Come now, and let us reason together, saith the LORD: though your sins be as scarlet, they shall be as white as snow; though they be red like crimson, they shall be as wool.   Isaiah 1:18

Running from Club to Club

I ran from club to club, trying to lose the pain, only to find more pain and also to hurt even more a family that was already hurting, just as I was. Then, just like Mary Magdalene, I came to a point in my life where I was so down that I thought the only way out was to take my life. And I was deadly serious.

I planned it all out. I would overdose on drugs. I first sat down and wrote a letter to each of my children, the children I had already hurt so much because I couldn't deal with my own pain. To escape my own pain, I was about to inflict even more pain on them.

> *When we get caught up in drugs and alcohol, we quickly lose our moral bearing!*

Why?

As I look back now, I can see why divorce tore me apart as it did, but I didn't understand it at the time. I was still carrying the baggage of having been molested by several grown men before the age of six, being abandoned as a child and witnessing far too much domestic abuse. My Hell had begun long before my divorce. Having to stand helplessly by as my father beat our mother time and time again had left a deep scar in my mind and emotions. Then, on top of that, seeing your own mother so full of pain and rejection that she turned into a drunkard was devastating.

People in our neighborhood sometimes would not allow their children to play with us because they considered us to be little more than "white trash." I remember particularly one day when Diane and I went next door (I was about six or seven) to play with a little neighbor girl. Before long, her mother came out and told her that she couldn't play with us because we were "nothing more than white trash." Diane took me by the hand, and we walked home together. I didn't fully understand the woman's words at the time, but Diane did.

Just like that, the foundation for the cycles of our life had been put into motion. It was not because of anything we had done, but what our parents had done and were doing. Yet, as so often happens, it's the children who pay the price.

Then there was being left alone at home night after night, days at a time, before the age of twelve and then having the State step in, wanting to take me away. Again, it wasn't for anything I had done, but rather something my parents had done, but that didn't make it any easier. Then, on top of all that, I reached out to grab onto a man, who would also leave me one day—just like everyone else had.

Someone To Love Me Forever

When I was pregnant with my first child at the age of fifteen, I was ecstatic. Now I would have someone who would love me and never leave me. She would be a baby girl, and I called her Michelle. She could never leave me because she belonged to me. My children would be mine forever.

But these were the thoughts of a little girl who didn't know how to grow up. Through my marriage, I had tried to find the childhood I'd never had. What a rude awakening I received when eventually Michelle, my daughter, my life, also left me. This was the one person I had thought would never go away, and now she had, choosing to live with her father who had left us. I couldn't understand why she would choose to go live with him, and I was devastated by her departure, so caught up in self pity that I couldn't see that she was hurting more than me. I was blinded by my hurts and couldn't see past my own pain. As the all-too-true saying goes: Hurting people hurt other people.

The hardest thing I had to do, in all of this, was not just to forgive others, but also to forgive myself. It took me a very long time to do that. Jesus forgives us as soon as we ask. Then we just have to forgive ourselves.

Then two more of my children left. This time it was due to my own mistakes, but at the time all I could see was that life was over for me. Everyone I loved was abandoning me, one by one. At that point, continuing to live in this world was more than I could bear. Before it was over, I had sent the rest of the children to their father, for I was suddenly a basket case. My mind had been ripped apart, just like my heart and my soul.

> *I stopped praying for a very long time and started running!*

I must add here that although I was devastated when Brandy, my youngest daughter, also went to live with her dad, I later realized that it had been for her good. After I had come to know the Lord, I heard some studies on Christian television that showed that girls who were raised with the presence of a father in the home were less likely to become sexually promiscuous at a young age, and therefore the presence of a father was a major deterrent to teenage pregnancy. When I heard that, I stopped worrying about Brandy and committed the matter to the Lord, and, sure enough, she did well being raised by her dad.

Now, let's continue with our journey.

The Only Prayer I Knew

At twenty-nine, this little Catholic girl was praying the only prayer she had known until then. It was from childhood:

Now I lay me down to sleep.
I pray the Lord my soul to keep.
If I should die before I wake,
I pray the Lord my soul to take.

I always added a phrase asking to God bless everyone in our family. I had prayed this prayer every night until the divorce, but then I stopped praying for a very long time and started running. I ran for years ... until that night in 1984, when I was about to end this Hell on earth. It had gone on far too long.

I got all dressed up, wrote the good-bye letters to my children, believing the lie of Satan, that somehow they would be better off without me. I did take time to ask Jesus to forgive me for what I was about to do. I was tired of drinking and doing drugs to dull my pain, and I couldn't find a way to put my family back together again. Our home was destroyed, and the children were gone. Everything had been stripped from me, one piece at a time. I was sliding deeper and deeper into Hell, and I felt that I had tried everything I knew to change it all. But no one seemed to have an answer for me.

I Got the Pills Out

I got the drugs out and placed them on the bed, and I was about to take them ... when suddenly there was a knock at the bedroom door. The boyfriend of the lady friend, with whom I was living at the time, was there. He had become like a brother to me, but he never came to my bedroom door. Now he was saying, "Jody, are you all right?"

"I'm fine," I assured him, and he went away. I often thought how strange it was for him to ask about me at that very moment.

My mind went back to a time years before when, at sixteen, I had been expecting my second child. I had tried to take my life then too. The spirit of suicide had been heavy upon me. I loved the father of my unborn child, but he was in the Air Force and had been sent overseas. I wrote him every day, but was disappointed that he never answered.

Eventually I wrote to the chaplain to inquire about his welfare and to see just what was going on. Probably at the chaplain's insistence, he answered me at long last, but his answer was not what I wanted to hear. Instead, he sent me what is sometimes called a "Dear Helen" letter, or some refer to it as a "Dear John" letter. He wasn't ready to settle down, he said. He was sorry, but he had to say good-bye.

I vaguely remember driving to the bridge, and then I was told later that I had jumped into the water below. I do remember the sound of angels singing, and then someone pulled me out of the water. Then I was lying on the beach, spitting up saltwater.

In the years to come, I learned to push bad events like this one down deep into my mind and heart, so that I could survive from day to day. We learn quickly how to hide our pain and the things we don't want to face. But now it had all come rushing back so that life seemed unbearable and death a welcome escape.

A Second Attempt

My mind was now back in the room. I would again attempt to take the pills. Then my friend knocked on the door again, and then someone was knocking on the front door. Of all things, it was a Baptist Sunday school teacher.

My girlfriend's children went to that church on Sunday mornings. Like many, she was drinking, taking drugs and living with a man she wasn't married to, and yet she always wanted her children to go to church. I suppose that makes people think that they're not so bad. They're wrong, of course.

But how good God is! He always sends someone to help us get our feet on the right pathway, and He had sent this fine lady. But all I could think about was trying to get rid of her as fast as possible. I had matters to attend to—life and death matters.

Then, in the middle of all this, the guy I was dating at the time showed up at the door. So there we were, a bunch of sinners from the world, talking to a Baptist Sunday school teacher.

In later years, I often wondered if that lady was from the local church or not. Was she perhaps an angel sent to delay me and prevent me from taking my life?

My Dream

As everyone talked, my mind went back to a dream I'd been having every night for the past three nights. It was the same thing every time, over and over again.

In the dream, I was standing at a fork in the road and would have to either go left or right. To my left, was a wide road. It looked like it had rubies on it. The lights were so bright, and I could hear the sound of music playing, the kind of music I liked to dance to.

The much smaller road to my right was very dim and not at all appealing to the eye. It looked more like a dirt path than an actual road. I couldn't see down it, and I didn't hear any music.

After I'd had the same dream for several nights in a row, I remember thinking, *I need a Bible.* That seemed like a joke. I had never read a Bible in my life. I did have a big family Catholic Bible, and I had looked at the pictures in it a few times. But now it was packed away, along with all my hopes and dreams, in a different state. I had thought of it again that day, before everyone moved in to ruin the one thing I thought I could do right—take my life.

I wanted the Bible because I didn't want to go to Hell. I had heard Mom say, "People who take their life go straight to Hell." I wanted to die, but I didn't want to go to Hell. I had enough problems already without that. I climbed up to the top of an old book shelf, and there I found a Bible under an inch of dust. I wiped it off and went and climbed back into bed.

I took a deep breath, and then I asked the Lord to forgive me for what I was about to do and to please understand. I reminded Him of all that was wrong in my life and why I was about to do this thing people called suicide. Then I opened the Bible, just to see for myself what it said.

I had spent years messing up my life, and now I was also messing up my way out of it!

A Great Adventure

It was a great adventure for this little Catholic girl. I noted immediately all the *thees* and *thous*, and then, to top it all off, I noticed that the Bible was telling something about grasshoppers. Grasshoppers? What was that doing in the Bible? Was this a book of fairy tales or what? I closed the Bible, put it aside and slept, and once again I had the dream, needing to decide which way to go.

Now here I was sitting in the living room with a drug user, a man who was lusting after my body and a Baptist Sunday school teacher, and we were all talking. What was a basket case like me doing in a conversation like this? Let's face it: it hadn't been a very good day. I had spent years messing up my life, and now I was also messing up my way out of it.

There has to be more than this to life, I thought as I sat there pondering this predicament. Then the phone rang. It was my sister Diane. The Lord had shown a friend of hers that I was about to take my life. Diane didn't say that at the time. She just asked me if I would go to church with her that night. She would come and get me and bring me home again.

But that didn't make sense. Diane didn't live on the other side of town. She lived three hours away.

I told her to give me a minute to think it over, and then I turned to the man who was lusting after me and asked him what he thought about it. He said I should go, so I told her I would. *I might as well go,* I thought. I wasn't making any headway with my plans.

As I look back on it all now, I can see Jesus in everything that happened that day. He was there, fighting for my life. He was with me. There can be no doubt. It was not my appointed time for death, as I had thought, but rather it was my appointed time for salvation.

My Appointment with Salvation

It's hard to believe now, but after Diane came and was talking to me, I sat on my bed smoking a marijuana joint. She began telling me about Jesus and how much He loved me, and she continued to talk about Him after we got in the car and were on our way. She said that He had a purpose for me. *Imagine that,* I thought, *the Creator of the entire universe has things for me to do for Him—me, Jody, the loser, so wrapped up in self-pity that I couldn't see anything else.*

I listened for a while to what she was saying, and then I told her, "I'll go to church with you, but I'm not going to be one of those 'rollie pollies.' " It was my way of saying Holy Rollers. I had heard people speak in tongues a few times when I was small, but I had decided that it just wasn't for me. Just in case it was from God, I wasn't going to say anything bad about it, but, again, it wasn't for me. Of that I was sure.

I didn't know a lot about God "stuff," but I certainly didn't want God mad at me. I had enough to deal with already.

By the time we got to Diane's house, she was tired. Mom was there, and she was telling Diane that she should rest. We could go to church the next night.

Diane was looking down, and she suddenly saw a little bug, one of the kind we always called a rollie pollie bug. Then she remembered what I had said in the car about not being willing to become one of those 'rollie pollies.' She said to the Lord, "Is this a sign? Does this mean that you're going to save Jody and fill her with the Holy Spirit?" Then, convinced that this was, indeed, a sign from God, she jumped up and said to me, "We're going NOW!" And off we went to church.

On the way, Diane was talking about God, and silently I was talking to Him. She didn't know what I told Him. It was: "If everything she's said is true, and You really need me to do something for You, if You really have some purpose for me, then here I am."

> *The next thing I knew I was dancing all over that church!*

My mind wanted to dwell on the question of speaking in tongues, for Diane had told me again about the Holy Spirit and His work. He would take me just as I was, she said. But my heart said, "All I have to offer is my heart." I had nothing else left under my control. "I'm nothing," I said, "but here I am. If You want me, I'm Yours."

Then I added, "About the tongues 'stuff,' I want everything that's real and of You." That was a very big step for a little Catholic woman.

A Very Plain Little Building

We arrived at the church. It was a very plain little building, with a lot of people in it. The women all wore long dresses and no makeup, and I stood out like a sore thumb in my bright red dress cut about five inches above the knee. If that wasn't bad enough, it had slits up the sides.

I walked in and sat down, and then I waited to see what was going to happen next—not with the people, but with Jesus. I was sure that He had something planned.

I didn't know enough about the things of God to realize that I just asked Him to come into my heart in the car. I had felt something warm inside when I was talking to Him, but now I was expecting something to take place. I just wasn't sure what.

Before long, a little man with a red bow tie on got up and began talking about grasshoppers, of all things, in the Bible. He had my full attention, for I remembered what I had read from the Bible back at the house. I knew then that something good was about to happen, and I felt trust for this man. Whatever he said I could believe.

The man's name was Brother Charles, and he was a true man of God, I was about to learn. He suddenly stopped preaching and told Diane to bring me to the front. Later she told me she was thinking, "Oh, no, Lord! If he says something to Jody, she'll walk out." But, to her surprise, I stood up, and together we walked to the front.

All I remember Brother Charles doing that night was speaking in a strange language and placing his hand on my head. But the next thing I knew I was dancing all over that church.

At one point, I turned my head to Diane and said, "We're going to dance our way to Heaven." She looked at me and smiled, and then everyone in the church started clapping and praising God. I didn't understand, at first, what they were so happy about. I thought I had spoken to Diane in English, but I hadn't. I was speaking in another language.

Just that quickly, Jesus had heard and answered my prayer. In an instant's time, I was born-again and filled with the Holy Spirit—with the evidence of speaking in other tongues. Diane wasn't able to understand a word I said, but she knew that Jesus had filled me with the Holy Spirit.

For my part, I just couldn't stop dancing. I felt so wonderful, so clean, so alive, like I had my whole life ahead of me. I knew in that moment that my life would now be different. I was a new person, and I had purpose.

It was very difficult for me to fall asleep that night. I was so happy that the tears of joy just wouldn't stop flowing.

The Same Dream Again

When I did finally get to sleep, I had the same dream again. This time there was a difference. I was again standing at the same crossroad, trying to decide which way to go. The wide road to my left had its bright red rubies, its bright lights and its good music, and the little dirt path to my right was dimly lit. And yet instinctively I started walking to my right, toward the little dirt path.

When I did this, I heard a loud sound behind me and

turned just in time to see some big black gates closing. Now the ruby red road wasn't rubies at all, but flames of fire. Thank God! I was on the other side of the gates, walking toward the little path.

As I started down that path, I saw that it wasn't dirt at all. It was gold. And the dim light got brighter and brighter. I knew then that this path would take me to Heaven. I had made the right choice.

That wide road had led to Hell, and this path would take me to Heaven. It had been my last chance to get saved, and it was only by the grace of God that I had asked Jesus into my life that night.

I stood in a little church that night, alive for the first time in years, born again, instead of lying somewhere in a morgue, dead from suicide. The choice had been mine. Thank God that He kept putting people in my way that day. I wondered if that Baptist Sunday school teacher was still there. I wanted to go back and tell her how God had used her, along with the others, to save not only my life, but also my soul. Jesus had protected me that day and spared me from a burning Hell forever.

Mary Knew this Kind of Hell

Mary Magdalene knew this kind of Hell too. I'm sure of it. She heard that Jesus was with the Pharisees, but she didn't care who was with Him or what they might think. She knew enough to realize that she wouldn't be welcomed by them, but she was ready to risk everything for the chance to be made clean. She was at the end of her rope. She, too, stood at a crossroad, just like me—and maybe you too.

Mary was a woman who had made many mistakes in life, but now she just walked right in and sat down at Jesus' feet, and as she wept, her tears fell on his feet. There were so many of those tears that she felt she had to somehow dry His feet, but she had nothing to dry them with. So she used her own hair. That day, Mary Magdalene also found forgiveness and purpose for her life.

How Pure!

I can't put into words how pure I felt that day, and I don't think Mary could either. The feeling of such purity to a person who has felt dirty for so long is something very wonderful. You've been lost, and suddenly you're found. You felt like you had nothing to live for, but now you have a whole new life ahead—and all because of a man named Jesus. He took the time to care, to forgive and, yes, to die, so that people like Mary Magdalene and Jody Amato and, yes, you could start over with a clean slate, forgiven, with every sin washed away by His blood.

Who would think that a woman with an alabaster box whose name was Mary would find a special place at Jesus' feet? And who would think that a woman named Jody, with nothing at all in her hand to offer except an open heart to receive the Lord, would one day be going into churches, preaching the Gospel of Jesus Christ and seeing captives set free—or writing a book about her wonderful Savior Jesus Christ? How good the Lord is!

If the Shoe Fits ...

If Mary's slipper fits your foot, you're ready to give up and Hell is pulling you to the point of no return, know that Jesus is very real, and so is the salvation He offers to you today. Allow Him to place that slipper of salvation upon your lost and dying soul, and you, too, can dance you way to Heaven.

Amen!

Chapter 10

The Woman at the Well's Slipper

*He said to her, "Go, call your husband and come here."
The woman answered and said, "I have no husband."
Jesus said to her, "You have correctly said, 'I have no
husband'; for you have had five husbands, and the
one whom you now have is not your husband; this
you have said truly."*   John 4:16-18, NAS

As we near the end of our journey, there are still
many women of the Bible with a story to tell, but we
cannot forget the woman at the well. She was a Samaritan, and, again, we don't know her name.

A Story Worth Telling

And why is this woman's story worth telling? It's worth

telling because she knew shame. Hers was the same kind of shame that affects many modern-day women—shame that the divorce rate is as high as it is in our country, shame that we've personally been married more than once, or shame that we've gone from relationship to relationship and seen them all fall apart. Today many women have had several husbands or, at the very least, several relationships, and we need to meet Jesus at the well.

Cruel Words

This woman had been through five husbands, and the man she was living with at the time was not her husband. She was so ashamed of her life and how it had gotten to that point that she would wait until the heat of the day to go to the well to get water. I'm sure this was so that she wouldn't meet other women and have to listen to them making fun of her.

People can be very cruel, and it's always a sad thing when we're already feeling that life has beaten us down, and then people around us, even family members, begin to make fun of how many times we've been married or how many men we've known. That's why the Samaritan woman learned to avoid being around people. They, no doubt, joked or made little remarks like:

"What number is this?"
"Are you still with the same man?"
"I can't keep up with your last name changes?"

To you, it's not funny, not funny at all. Their snide remarks are just a reminder of all your broken dreams. And the number just represents how many times you desperately tried to make a relationship work, but then it failed anyway.

People who make jokes like these don't see all the tears and rejection you have battled over the years. Most of them would never have fought as hard as you did to make a relationship work. They would have thrown in the towel within the first six months, but you kept trying. You just wanted someone to accept you the way you were, someone who could see your heart and know the truth about your life. It was not just a number for you—never a number.

So, like the woman at the well, you try to hide the pain and the shame, by pulling away from being included. You don't know what it is to feel accepted, only exploited. If other people would only reach out to you in love instead of always criticizing you!

This woman had been through five husbands, and the man she was living with at the time was not her husband!

Not Very Young

Somehow I don't believe that the woman at the well was still a young person, but I have no proof of that. I know some who, before the age of sixteen, have had two husbands, one who, before the age of thirty-one, had three husbands, and one who had five husbands before the age of thirty-five. Many women have such deep emotional scars from so many broken relationships that they've come to the conclusion that only a certain type of man can take care of them. It's sad to see them so mixed up.

These are not only the lost of which I speak. Many Christians fail in marriage because they have not allowed Jesus to heal them from the hurts of the past. As a consequence, they're unable to build a mature relationship with their mate. Some Christians think, *"This is it. I'm saved now, so whoever I marry, I'll be happy."* And they, too, fail. It takes time to be healed, and, as we have noted before, not every man who comes along is God's chosen mate for us.

Lives Filled with Junk

My sister Diane once told me that the Lord showed her something important. She had not built up all of this pain in her life in one day, and so it would not be removed in one day either. The Lord showed her a big junk pile, and things began to come off of that junk pile one at a time. That's how some healings and restorations must take place—one piece at a time.

Tired of Being Alone

As we noted in an earlier chaper, most of us jump from one relationship to another simply because we don't want to be alone. We are, too often, willing to settle for less than God's best for our lives and less than we want and need ourselves—and all because we're tired of the single life.

Some are tired of having to live with a parent, and they think they need more freedom. They don't realize that along with what they call "freedom" comes bills that have to be paid. If they choose that "freedom," they suddenly discover that they can't "run the roads" anymore. Instead, they have to work to pay the bills and be able to eat. And they get very tired of working all those hours.

On Friday night, when all their friends are going out, they have to work to pay the light bill, or the electricity will be turned off. Then the thought comes, *"If I just had a husband, he would take care of me."* And they're headed for another broken relationship—even before it starts. Why? Because their motive for considering marriage is wrong. This is not what marriage is all about.

Some are divorced, and then, before long, they find themselves being drawn to exactly the same type of man. I did this more than once. I had been raised to think that a woman always needed a man to take care of her, but this was years ago—when people stayed married no matter what happened.

Forced to Marry

When I was just fifteen, Mom told me I had to get married. She couldn't afford to take care of me anymore.

> *I had dreams of finishing school, getting a job and eventually becoming an airline stewardess!*

I wasn't at all sure that marriage was what I wanted just then. I had dreams of finishing school, getting a job and eventually becoming an airline stewardess. But, since get married was what I was told I had to do, that's what I did. But the marriage was doomed from the beginning. He was in his twenties, and I was just a little girl.

Children are often forced into relationships by parents who are not providing them with a Christian home. The children, for their part, are, too often, quick to jump at the chance to marry. Sometimes it's because of drugs or alcohol, but more often it's simply because they're hurting. Their own family is falling apart, and they desperately need someone to hold them, someone to make them feel that everything's all right. So they run into the first outstretched set of arms and to the first man who says, "I love you, and I will never leave you." More often than not, it's all a lie. And the enemy is just setting them up for a fall. How sad it is!

Grabbing onto the First Person who Comes Along

Hurting people have the tendency of grabbing onto the first person who comes along. They're frightened and seem to be falling into some unseen pit. What happens then is that they pull the other person down with them.

When I was first faced with divorce, I hated the thought. Satan taunted me, "There's no forever in marriage. It was all a big joke." Then, after a while, I no longer knew what the word *commitment* meant, and my heart was so hardened that I could no longer love. When I entered into any relationship, I always thought, "If it doesn't work out, I can always get a divorce." I told one man to his face, "You can be replaced," and I meant it.

Such a hardened heart brings pain, not only to you, but also to people around you. When you hear anyone talking like that, always remember that no one is born with that kind of heart. It takes years of great pain to turn clay to stone. Jesus, by the grace of God, can do the reverse—turning stone into soft, flexible putty.

Before that first divorce, I was thought of as a very tender and easygoing person. I was very loving, meek and gentle. But then the life of Hell began to take its toll on me, and, before long, I was no longer gentle or kind. I just knew that I was hurting, and I had to put on a tough face—or someone else would hurt me.

Unloved and Unloving

I began to think that if I didn't love anyone then I couldn't be hurt. And a greater lie began to form in my mind: No one loved me—not my children, not a man, maybe not even God.

But I didn't give God much thought most of the time. I was just too busy trying to survive in life. Thank God that He didn't neglect me. He sent His Son, Jesus Christ, to die for me, and then He reached into Hell and pulled me out. He washed away the tears and dirt, and I found true love for the first time in my life.

Jesus didn't stop there. He filled me with the Holy Spirit and began, not only to heal my heart, but also to reveal my heart to me so that I could see all the junk. It had built up over the years and caused me to run from man to man. Now I could run from glory to glory with Jesus.

Jesus Came to the Well

Jesus came to the well that day, and that changed everything. The woman thought it was going to be just another day of shame. Little did she know that her life was about to be turned around.

When Jesus spoke to her and asked her for a drink, she must have felt untrusting at first. After all, He was a Jew, and Jews didn't have anything to do with Samaritans, considering that the Samaritan people were beneath them. So she had good reason to wonder where this conversation was headed. But Jesus had asked her for a drink, so she gave it to Him.

Next He asked her, "Where is your husband?" And she told him that she didn't have a husband.

"You answered truthfully," Jesus told her, but what He said next must have sent shock waves coursing through her mind. "You've had five husbands, and the man you're living with now is not your husband."

Who was this Man? How did He know her shameful history? And what did He want from her?

Some Christian Women Are Also Guilty

There are Christian women reading this book who are, even now, living with a man you're not married to. You're tired of being alone and lonely, tired of not having someone to love, tired of your children not having a father. You're tired of not having a hand to hold and tired of watching other couples kiss, when you don't even have anyone to talk to.

Many people end up in bad relationships simply because someone is better than no one—or so they think. That's always a wrong reason for entering into a relationship, but if that's you today, you can come to Jesus, at the well of living water. Just as He knew all this woman had done and yet He offered her the hope of something better in life, He extends His love to you today. You don't have to remain in the place of shame or of pain. It doesn't matter how many times you've been married or how many other relationships you've had. Jesus is offering you hope and healing today, and yes, a new beginning.

He Is Everything You Need

The Lord will bring you, as He did me, into a place that He becomes everything you need. I told Him, just a few months ago, that He was the best husband I'd ever had. He pays my bills, and He gave me a nice place to live, and it's all paid for.

One day I told the Lord, "I wish I had some diamonds." Before long a woman came to me and said, "The Lord told me to give this to you." It was a fine diamond ring. I had also asked for a bracelet with sapphires and diamonds, and she also gave me one of those.

I told my children about those wonderful blessings, and then one day a UPS truck stopped in front of the house with a package for me. My daughter had sent me a pair of diamond earrings and a diamond necklace. The enclosed note said, "This is to add to your diamond collection."

When the air-conditioner went out in my car, a mechanic said he would fix it—for free. When the central air-conditioning unit failed at my house, the Lord sent someone to my door with a check for a thousand dollars. They said, "An air-conditioning man is coming to put in a new unit for you, and here's the money to pay him." I'm not serving Jesus so that He'll bless me. I serve Him because He saved me, but He does take care of me.

The Lord told me, when I became single the last time, not to worry, that He would take care of me, and He has. He brought me through a bout with cancer, healing me, just as He promised He would.

I began to have problems with my lungs and was in the hospital for nine days and came home on oxygen. Again He healed me.

I had two heart catheters, but now I'm completely off of heart medication. (I will elaborate more on these miracles in the next chapter.)

> *The Lord will bring you, as He did me, into a place that He becomes everything you need!*

The List of Miracles Goes On

My list of miracles goes on and on. This is only what the Lord has done for me during the past two years. With Jesus, every battle brings a new blessing, through His wonderful power and what He did for me at Calvary. And it can be the same with you. Each of your battles can bring more and more of His wonderworking power into your life.

I thank God that I have not had to fight a single battle alone. He promised me that all my battles are His battles. And pity the person or the demon who tries to "mess" with God.

As Christians, we still have battles, but there's a big difference. Because we have Jesus, we have the hope and the expectation that everything will be all right. But ours is more than an expectation; it's an assurance that we will win the victory.

Her Shame Forgotten

Jesus asked the woman of Samaria for a drink of water from that natural well, but He gave her to drink of the well of living waters. That accomplished, she ran off excitedly to begin telling others about this amazing Man she had met who knew all that was in her heart, and yet He loved her.

In that moment, she forgot about all her shame, and she shared openly with everyone she met. This Man had accepted her as she was, and, in return, she had accepted Him as Lord and Savior of her life.

Somehow I think of this woman as the sum of all the others we have looked at thus far. With her many relationships, she sums up the doubts and fears of everyone. She, more than others, had worn a lot of slippers in life, a life lived with so many different men, and I therefore see in her, not just the woman at the well, but also perhaps Leah, Abigail, Bathsheba, Ruth, the woman with the issue of blood, Mary Magdalene and many more. You might want to add your name to that list.

If the Shoe Fits ...

If the woman at the well's slipper fits your foot, allow Jesus, not only to place the slipper of healing and deliverance from shame and regret on your foot, but also to anoint you. Just as she ran and began telling others all about this Man named Jesus (how He had told her all that she had done, and how He had living water to offer), you, too, can go forth in His power and anointing, to bring healing to others just like yourself.

Jesus is at the well today, and He's looking for a woman like you, someone He can love through, touch through and flow through. Are you ready to be His hands and His voice, to share His heart with some hurting person just like yourself? He is offering you more than a slipper today; He is offering you His sandals. If you are willing to walk in His shoes, just say yes to Him now.

Amen!

Chapter 11

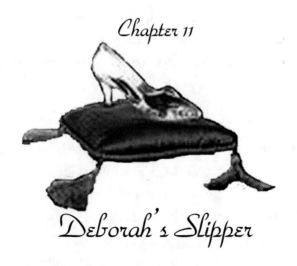

Deborah's Slipper

Now Deborah, a prophetess, the wife of Lappidoth, was judging Israel at that time.   Judges 4:4, NAS

This time, rather than travel forward in time, we must step back—way back. When I had reached this point in the writing of the book, the Spirit showed me that I had overlooked someone very important.

We find her in the book of Judges, among the palm groves, somewhere between Bethel and Ramah, north of Jerusalem. She was a prophetess named Deborah, and she was a woman of extraordinary knowledge and wisdom. Her fellow Israelites, from all the various tribes and regions, would come to consult with her in order to settle any disputes they had with one another. She could hear the voice of the Lord, she was instructed by the Spirit and was gifted in being able to interpret, or understand, what He wanted done or said in a given situation. She was the first and only woman placed in that position of authority, as judge over all of Israel. In this way, she represents women of every century in ministry.

Battles Go with Ministry

Deborah was a woman who knew how to war with her enemies!

There was something else unique and important about Deborah. She was a woman who knew how to war with her enemies:

Now she sent and summoned Barak the son of Abinoam from Kedesh-naphtali, and said to him, "Behold, the LORD, the God of Israel, has commanded, 'Go and march to Mount Tabor, and take with you ten thousand men from the sons of Naphtali and from the sons of Zebulun. I will draw out to you Sisera, the commander of Jabin's army, with his chariots and his many troops to the river Kishon, and I will give him into your hand.' "

Judges 4:6-7, NAS

As it turned out, Barak was afraid to go without Deborah, so she went with him and was largely responsible for the victory that came. Not only was she the judge over Israel; she was also the chief defender of the people. We'll look at this more a little later in the chapter.

Isn't it interesting that battles always seem to go with responsibility and ministry? You won't find the one without the other. Not all of us do well in battle, and sometimes we're left wounded and bleeding in the process.

You may have been called by the Lord into a great ministry, just like Deborah. But then something happened to make you feel that you had missed your chance, and you're now concerned that you're too broken or too old or that too much time has gone by for you to answer the call. But if you're reading this, it's not too late. I have seen great women of God go from battle to battle and, by the grace of God, move forward from being a victim to becoming a victor. You are a soldier in an army that has never lost a war, nor has it seen defeat. Rise up, mighty woman of God.

These words may well find you living among the ashes of your former life. I've seen gifted women walking for a time in such a mighty anointing that you had to stand back in awe at what God was doing through them. That He would empower someone in that way was truly amazing. Later, however, they were found fallen in the great heat of battle.

I Can Picture It

I can picture it in my mind even as I'm writing. I see a battlefield. Bombs are falling all around, and dust is flying into the air. Women, the victims of this battle, are being wounded and falling all around me. Suddenly a woman dressed in full armor comes through the fire left by the exploding bombs.

She is dressed in a white robe, but she wears a girdle of truth about her waist. She has a helmet of salvation upon her head, and it sits straight and tall. She wears a breastplate of glorious righteousness, a shield of wondrous faith is held in one of her hands, and a mighty sword is to be seen in the other. I see her moving forward, fighting the enemy with one hand and yet reaching down with the other hand to pick up a wounded and fallen sister.

She holds this sister around the waist, and her feet are dragging, and yet this woman of valor doesn't let go. She pushes forward, swinging her sword from left to right with her free hand. You can hear the battlecry of her heart and soul, as her voice sings out, "I am a soldier in the army of God, the most High."

Then, from an unseen direction, comes an unexpected blow from the enemy. It hits her so hard that this great anointed warrior falls to one knee and then to the ground. Now severely wounded, she is unable to lift herself up out of the ashes of the battlefield—much less help anyone else. Beloved, I believe that this woman is you.

You Were Raised Up

Whether or not you were molested as a child, whether

or not you did drugs or drank, whether or not you were beaten or abandoned or know the ravages of divorce or the trauma of having an abortion, at some point, God raised you up and thrust you out into the frontlines of ministry.

But then what happened somewhere along the way? What happened to that dynamic ministry you had? Where did the fire go? Where is that great battlecry that was once planted deep within your spirit, your mind and your heart?

Honey, it's still there—the gifts, the fire and the anointing. You haven't lost anything God has for you. Something happened that day or night that brought you to your knees, and it seemed to bring your vision and dreams down on the battlefield with you, but hold on. Help is on the way.

I Know the Heat of Battle

I know what it is to battle the enemy of life, for I've had many such battles, and they seem to come one after the other in quick succession. When I was already standing in the midst of what seemed like great destruction, the next battle would be upon me. But remember what the Lord said to Barak through Deborah about the enemy. *"I will give him into your hand."* Believe that God is about to do that same thing for you.

The Word of God teaches us that we overcome by the blood of the Lamb and the word of our testimony (see Revelation 12:11). I have many testimonies of victory in battle, and I want to share a few of them with you in the following pages so that you can see that God's love never fails and that we can overcome and continue to serve Him.

All the Slippers Fit Me

All the slippers of this book fit my life, and each one is a great testimony of, not only how the Lord delivered me, but also how He healed me. Just like you, I then found myself on the frontlines of ministry. But that was not the end of my battles. In fact, at that point, more and greater battles began. I was a woman of faith, a woman washed in the blood, a woman redeemed from the curse, and the enemy wanted to destroy me.

God gave me a strong deliverance ministry and enabled me to move in the gifts of the Spirit. I saw great signs and wonders following my ministry. Gold dust and feathers miraculously appeared in my meetings. People were healed, delivered and saved as I traveled to many places preaching God's Word and ministering His love.

I came to learn over the years, however, that in order to move forward into any new realm of the Spirit one must take new territory. A new mantle just means that you have learned to stand and fight at a new level, and you must fight until that particular battle is won. You may be knocked down at some point, but you get up again. You may be wounded in the battle, but you persevere and press on.

"To Kill Your Son"

I know what it is to be in the middle of a great battle and then to hear the Lord say, "Jody, the enemy is coming to kill your son."

"What son?" I asked, for I have three sons.

The Lord didn't answer me, so all I knew to do was fast and pray and war in the Spirit with all that was within me. I took the promises of God's Word and spoke them over all my sons day and night, as the battle raged on. I prayed over them until a peace came to me, and the Lord said, "Jody I'm going to give you a miracle phone call." Then, I knew I had won the victory.

A week or two later the Lord woke me in the night and said, "Take the children to Louisiana to your mother's." (After I was saved, some of my children came back to live with me.) I had only ten dollars, but it was enough to get gasoline, so I took the two children who were home at the time and drove to my mother's.

I was there only about an hour when the phone rang,

> *God gave me a strong deliverance ministry and enabled me to move in the gifts of the Spirit!*

and someone was on the line telling me that my son Tony had fallen from the fourth floor of a college building in New York and landed on concrete. His leg was broken in thirty-six places, his nose was gone, and the rest of his face was badly damaged. Doctors were saying they would have to amputate his leg.

This broke a mother's heart. Tony was only eighteen years old. I told them to please wait, not to take his leg just yet. I would come there as quickly as I could.

Mom agreed to keep the children and gave me the money to fly to New York. I had obeyed the Lord by going to her house, and now He had everything ready for me. His Word declares that He knows what we need even before we ask Him (see Matthew 6:8).

"I Spared Your Son's Life"

I remember sitting on the plane, talking to God, my eyes filled with tears. I was devastated by what had happened, and I didn't understand it. "Lord," I said, "I thought You told me You were going to give me a miracle phone call."

"I did, Jody," He answered. "I spared your son's life." In that moment, a peace that passes all understanding came over me, and I knew that my son would live and walk and talk again. He would recover from this terrible fall.

Forty-five minutes after the phone call came, I was on my way to New York, and three hours later, I was with Tony in his hospital room.

The battle had just begun, and I knew I had to keep praying in the Spirit. We can never stop praying when we get a breakthrough. We just keep on praying and believing until we get through.

I Needed Someone to Pray for Me

By the time I arrived at the hospital, they had decided not to amputate Tony's leg just yet. They would wait a few more hours to see if they could get some circulation back into it and keep it flowing. I still had peace, but I stayed day and night by his side, leaving only for short times to go to a nearby sunroom when the nurses came in to change his bandages.

I remember telling the Lord, "I'm strong in Spirit, but my body is very tired. I need someone to pray with me."

I had to keep praying, because the enemy was still trying to come against Tony in many different ways. He was not out of the woods yet by a long shot. In fact, his life was still on the line. If I could keep praying, he would be all right, but I would have to keep praying, so I needed someone to pray for me.

I tried looking in the phone book for a Spirit-filled church. I found one and left a message on their answering machine, but no one ever called me back.

Again, I prayed about my need. I was so very tired, because I'd had no sleep, and now I said to the Lord, "I really need someone to pray with me." And He heard my cry.

God is so good! Honey, if there are no born-again Christians to pray with you, God will just save someone and fill them with the Holy Spirit so they can do it. And that's what He did for me in that hospital.

> *At one point, I found myself in the hospital, hooked up to a twenty-foot oxygen line!*

Revival in the Sunroom

In the sunroom that day the Lord spoke to me to go and sit by a certain lady, and I shared with her my testimony of how I got saved. After I had shared that with her, I asked her if she would like to receive Jesus into her heart. To my surprise, she said no.

I was stunned. Had I missed God so badly? Still in dismay, I got up to walk away, when I felt a tug on my shirt. I hadn't noticed the lady to my right. I turned to her now, and she said, "I would like to receive Jesus into my heart."

God's love never fails, and He never lets us down. There I was in a Catholic hospital, and He was working. (I rejoice to report that we will meet many wonderful Catholics in Heaven. Thank God that He's not about religion but about relationship.) God gave me a wonderful prayer partner that day.

I thought I was on fire for God, but this lady was *really* on fire. She began to share Jesus with others around the hospital, and during the hours and days to come, people kept coming to Tony's room to get me to come and pray for them so that they could receive Jesus as their Lord.

Some also needed healing, and I prayed for them. Within a few days, we had an army of new believers holding hands in the sunroom, praying together every day. To God be all the glory! Their faith strengthened me, and I was able to help them too.

Tony came through all of this with flying colors. Today he is as handsome as ever, and he doesn't have even a limp to show for the ordeal he went through. God is so faithful!

Hooked Up to Oxygen

More battles were to come. At one point, I found myself in the hospital, hooked up to a twenty-foot oxygen line. The doctor there told me that I would be on oxygen for the rest of my life. I told him that I was coming out of that hospital within a week because I'd had a vision. I saw my hospital bed and all the tubes running to it, but above the bed I saw a sign that read "NEVER AGAIN!" And that was God's promise to me.

I remember telling the Lord that I needed Him to give me strength so that I could rise up from my weakness and go around the hospital praying for other patients. He spoke to me and said, "Jody, I didn't bring you here for the patients; I brought you here for the staff." From that moment, He began saving doctors and nurses. Even the Baptist chaplain of the hospital was touched by the Holy Spirit.

God said that I would be out of that hospital within a week, and that's exactly what happened. Our promise from His Word is this:

For with God nothing shall be impossible. Luke 1:37

Not only can our Lord do impossible things, but He will.

A Cancerous Tumor

It was only a few months after that when I was told that I had a cancerous tumor, and I was scheduled for emergency surgery within a few days. When I got home from the doctor's office that day, I didn't call anyone. I just sat on my bed talking to God.

"I don't understand," I told the Lord. "But although I don't understand, I do trust You." And that was enough. I had a great peace about the whole matter.

Then the Lord said, "Jody, remember when I told you to show mercy to that person who had hurt you, and you did?"

I had to admit that when the Lord told me to show that person mercy, I hadn't really wanted to do it, but He had helped me. Now I said, "Yes, Lord."

He said, "Because you showed them mercy, I'm going to show you mercy now. I'm going to cut this thing out of your body and heal you. And then I will anoint you, and you will pray for others who have cancer and I will heal them too." I was so happy that I couldn't wait to tell the doctor. I wouldn't need the surgery after all because Jesus had healed me.

When I finally had a chance to tell the doctor, he wasn't nearly as excited as I was. He said, "Now, Mrs. Amato, we need to do this."

I thought about it for a while, and then I answered him, "All right, you've done your tests and your biopsy, and they showed cancer. So, go ahead with the surgery, but I can tell you right now that you won't find any cancer. By doing the surgery, you can document my healing."

He had other ideas, but when the surgery was done, and the results came back, no cancer had been found. The doctor was at a loss for words to explain what had happened. I knew. All glory be to our God!

Paul wrote to the Romans:

If God be for us, who can be against us?

Romans 8:31

It's a very good question.

Still the battles came, as I kept marching forward, running this race with patience, ever moving toward the mark of the high calling in Christ. And all along the way God was changing me on the inside, as well as on the outside. With every battle came growth and maturity and faith in the things I could not see.

Taken to the Third Heaven

In the midst of the battles, I had a lot of glorious experiences. For instance, I was speaking in a meeting in Amite, Louisiana, one bright Friday morning. The service had just started, and I went over to pray for a certain lady when she went down in the Holy Spirit—and so did I. This had never happened to me before.

I awakened standing in a white robe in a place I believed to be the third Heaven. Everything around me was also white. I saw large double doors and angels standing on each side of them.

Some men approached me and began patting me on the back. They were congratulating me, saying, "Well done!" I didn't know what they were talking about, but I did know who they were. One was Moses, and the others were Jesus' original disciples. They all sat down on a white bench that appeared to be made of stone, and I did the same.

I heard an angel call my name, so I got up and started walking toward the double doors. They opened, and to my wonder, there stood the Lord Himself in all His glory.

The room filled with bright light, and I could see that

the Lord was dressed in white, but there was such brightness that I could only make out His right hand, part of His arm and one sleeve of His robe. It was full and long.

He held out His hand to me and said, "I give to you the keys over death and Hell." It made me think of Jesus' words:

> *I will give you the keys of the kingdom of heaven; whatever you bind on earth will be bound in heaven, and whatever you loose on earth will be loosed in heaven.*
>
> Matthew 16:19, NIV

I said to Him, "Lord, if this is really happening to me, then when I go back, let the others see Your glory on my face, as Moses experienced. Then, in the blink of an eye, I was getting up off the floor in Amite.

> *The doors opened, and to my wonder, there stood the Lord Himself in all His glory!*

The meeting was over, and I was told that it went quite well. Most of the people had already gone, but two ladies were still at the front, packing up the equipment. They were my sister Diane and a dear friend who was my assistant at the time. As I stood up, the power of God hit the two of them, even though I hadn't said a word about seeing Jesus.

Did You See Anything?

Later that night, I had time to meditate on what I had seen and heard in Heaven. Then, around eleven that night, I was speaking with Diane and I asked her, "Did you see anything different when I got up off the floor this morning?"

She sat there for a moment, and then she told me what had happened. "When you were on the floor," she said, "I walked over to where you were and looked down at you, but somehow I felt that you were not really there. I asked the Lord, 'Where is she?' And the Lord said, 'She's with Me.' Then, when you stood up, your face was like the face of Moses. It was so bright that I couldn't see your features." Those words took my breath away. I had indeed seen the Lord Jesus face to face.

A Life-Threatening Infection

But when storms come to our lives, we often quickly forget our wondrous encounters with the Lord. Just two days after my trip to Heaven my oldest son, Danny, called and said that he had an unusual infection in his body. A doctor had told him that they didn't know what it was but that it actually appeared to be life-threatening. If they couldn't get it stopped, he might die.

When I hung up the phone, I sat there for what seemed like a very long time talking to God. "Is my son going to die?" I asked Him.

"Jody," He answered, "remember the keys I gave you. If you'll pray, I'll heal your son."

I prayed, but instead of getting better, Danny seemed to get worse. For the next several months, he was in and out of the hospital. I kept telling him, "You're going to be all right. Jesus is going to heal you. I promise."

They still were not sure what caused this terrible infection, but it was a serious one. Now it moved into his throat, and he called me, barely able to speak. When I answered the phone and heard his voice, barely above a whisper, saying, "Mom, Mom," my heart felt like it was being torn out of my chest. I could hear his tears and his fears.

With tears of my own, I said to him, "Baby, you're going to be okay. Jesus said so. He told me that if I prayed for you, He would heal you. Everything's going to be all right."

The next morning I awakened to find Satan standing at the foot of my bed. He said to me, "If you will step down from ministry and stop praying for souls to be saved, I will take my hands off of your son." For a split second, I could see Danny crying in pain and I felt his fear. It was a vision from the enemy. Then, suddenly, the righteousness of God rose up in me and I said to Satan in a very strong and authoritative voice, "Jesus Christ is the only hope my son has."

Tempted by the Devil

In that moment, I could relate to the time Jesus had been led, or drawn, by the Spirit into the wilderness to be tempted by Satan. When this happened, He stood victorious on the Word. After the enemy had finished all this tempting, *"he [Satan] left him [Jesus]"* (Luke 4:13, NLT). The very next thing that Luke recorded was the fact that *"Jesus returned to Galilee, filled with the Holy Spirit's power"* (Luke 4:14), and He now did more than ever.

> **Keys are a means of gaining or preventing entrance, possession, or control: an instrumental or deciding factor!**

Honey, you, too, are getting ready to walk in the power of the Holy Spirit like never before. You're about to mount up with wings as an eagle. No more will you hide in the clefts of despair, hopelessness, doubt, disbelief and fear when storms come. Instead, you will rise in the realm of the Spirit, so that you can soar above it all. Glory to God!

From that moment on, my son began to recover and was soon back to health. They never did discover what had caused the infection or what exactly it was, but I knew that it was just an attack from the enemy. Because of what Jesus did on the cross, we won the victory again.

What Are Keys?

So I had some keys. According to one Bible dictionary,

keys are "emblems of authority, opening and shutting at will the gates of Hades (Hell)." Another dictionary gives the meaning of keys as: a means of gaining or preventing entrance, possession or control, an instrumental or deciding factor." Honey, you hold the keys, so you decide what is bound on earth and what is loosed on earth. Jesus paid the price at the cross so that you could walk in this kind of authority.

Satan knows who you are, for he can see and smell the sweet scent of the blood of the Lamb in you and on you. He knew I had the authority to destroy and defeat his plans. His only hope was that I would fall for his lie, the lie that he had power over my son and over my life and ministry, and that I didn't have that power. And that's exactly what he's trying to do to you too. If you'll stand strong on God's promises, Satan won't succeed. You are a mighty woman of valor, and you not only have the keys. You also know how to use them.

Just like Deborah, you have many testimonies of victory. Think and meditate on your victories, never on any defeats. The Holy Spirit empowered Deborah over and over again to speak and act with authority, and He has empowered you in the same way.

Married Women in Ministry

Deborah knew what it was to be married and still be in ministry, for the Bible identifies her as a wife and names her husband. I've known many great women in ministry, and some of them have had wonderful husbands who encouraged them to walk out their calling and helped them to do it. Sadly, others have had a very different experience. When women feel that they have to wait for a husband to get saved or answer the call of God on their lives, many years can be lost. Well, Honey, if that's you, the wait is over. This is your day.

I know what it's like to watch the years go by and wonder when a husband will do the right thing. I was afraid to leave the house to go to church for fear that as soon as I left, he would be on the phone with another woman. I was right about what he would do in my absence, but staying home to guard the phone didn't change the fact that he was cheating on me.

A Repeated Vision

Over a period of four or five years, the Lord gave me a number of visions. I could see myself in a white outfit, and I could hear the Lord calling me to ministry. I would start walking toward Him, but then I would stop and turn, and I could see my husband standing in back of me. I would say to the Lord, "What about Him, Lord? Can he come with me?" Without the Lord saying a word, I knew I could wait a little longer. So each time, I turned and walked back toward my husband, and the vision ended.

A few years later, I had the same vision again on two different occasions. Then a third vision came, but this time it was different. As before, I was dressed in a white robe, and I was walking toward the Lord, seeing Him in His glory. The difference was that I suddenly heard my husband's voice calling out to me. He was saying, "Jody, what about me?"

Unlike the previous visions, this time I decided not to turn around and go back to him. Somehow I sensed that this was my final opportunity. If I went back now, the Lord would not call me again. So, as I went forward, my eyes on the Lord, I said, without even turning to look back, "Lord, what do You say?" I was asking Him what He wanted me to do. I was ready to say, like Jesus, *"Not My will, but Yours, be done"* (Luke 22:42, NKJ).

Every Husband Has a Choice to Make

The Lord spoke to me very tenderly in reference to my husband: "Jody, it's up to him. The choice is his. The scripture that came to me, as I kept walking toward Jesus, was from Paul's letter to the Philippians:

> *Wherefore, my beloved, as ye have always obeyed, not as in my presence only, but now much more in my absence, work out your own salvation with fear and trembling.* Philippians 2:12

Every man must work out his own salvation. So love your husband, and see that all of his and your children's needs are meet. Then kiss him on the head, and be on your way to do what the Lord has called you to do. When you get back home, share with him the wonderful things you've seen and heard. That's all you can do. The rest is up to him.

Far too many women are not in church because they're waiting on their husband to go with them. You can do this alone, great woman of destiny. Pray for him, and don't abandon him, but you have to go on about your Father's business. If you can't serve God with a husband, then you won't serve Him without one. The battles are still there. They're just different battles.

When your husband sees the gleam you have in your eyes when you come home and hears the laughter in your voice, and when he sees your caring and your tenderness, he just might come to desire what you have. But even if he doesn't take notice, Jesus does, and you'll have your joy back.

Some might insist, "Jody, you just don't understand. He won't let me go. When I try to go, he makes a scene or maybe even gets mean." I know a sister who had a husband who would beat her up every time she went to church. One day he picked her up by the throat and pushed her back against the wall. In that moment, something rose inside of her, and she was no longer afraid of him. She said to him, "You put me down right now, or Jesus is going to strike you dead." The fear of God got hold of that man, and now he not only lets her go to church; he has helped her get a church of her own so that she can fulfill the calling on her life to pastor.

Deborah's Heart

Deborah's heart was to do what I believe the heart of the Lord is for all women today as well: to help position men in their rightful place of leadership. Just as there are great men (and there are many), there are also great women—just like you. You have purpose, little one. If you could only see yourself through the Fathers eyes, you would never be the same again.

Deborah wanted Barak to step up, but when she told him the word the Lord had spoken, to go forward and fight, he wouldn't—not without her. So she went along, but she let him know that, because of the way he was handling this matter, the honor that would result from the upcoming victory would not go to him, but to a woman.

The Bible doesn't say if Barak thought the woman Deborah spoke of was herself or not, but it makes me wonder. I can somehow see him and his men, who may have overheard this conversation, think-

> *Deborah wanted Barak to step up, but when she told him the word the Lord had spoken, to go forward and fight, he wouldn't—not without her!*

ing that very thing. But it was another woman who would step up to the plate this time.

The Battle Was Easily Won

In the meantime, Deborah and her troops went forth to face the enemy, wondering how God would give such a great host into their hand. You might be thinking to yourself, "I'm nothing. I couldn't do anything great like Deborah. I'm not a pastor or an apostle. I haven't cast out any demons. I haven't even laid hands on anyone in a very long time." But you're wrong, so wrong. All that is required is that you be chosen and anointed by God, and I assure you that you are definitely one of His chosen ones.

A sudden, violent rainstorm flooded the Kishon River, turning the valley into a mud hole. In that mud, the great chariots of the enemy with their grand horses got bogged down. The Israelites then descended upon the helpless Canaanites and overpowered them. Thus, King Jabin's domination over the Israelites in the north ended.

But Sisera the captain of the host, fled on foot and sought refuge in the tent of a woman named Jael. God had said that Sisera would die, so what was He about to do through this woman?

The woman was just a housewife, the spouse of Heber the Kenite, not a prophetess nor a judge. To the enemy, she was nothing. Certainly she could not pose any threat to a man as great as Sisera, so he felt safe in her humble abode and decided to rest there until he could decide what to do next.

She Was Not Afraid

As humble as she was, Jael was not afraid of this powerful and important man. She actually ran out to meet him. This enemy may have been lining her up for a defeat, but she was going to have her say about it.

This little women had no great title, no license to preach, she wasn't ordained by men and she had no doctorate, but she, just like you and I, was called and anointed by the Lord for a specific purpose. It's time to get up and stop the enemy advance, so run to your destiny with all the authority God has given you.

Sisera asked Jael for something to drink, and she gave it to him and then gave him something to cover himself with so that he could rest. He told her to stand in the door of the tent, and if anyone was to ask if someone had come there, she was to tell them no. Isn't that just like the enemy, trying to pull us into sin after he has already attacked our self-esteem, our self-worth?

A God Plan

Sisera was asking Jael to lie, but she had another plan. And it was not just any plan; it was a God plan.

You may feel, at this point, that you don't know what

to do or how to do it. Get ready, for our Lord and Savior is about to give you a God plan for your life.

Jael picked up a tent peg and a hammer and went quietly to Sisera's side while he lay fast asleep, utterly exhausted. It's easy to see that she had determination and confidence, and I believe it was because she knew she was doing the will of God. She drove that peg right through his temple and into the ground, and he died without stirring.

This was a turning point in the battle against Canaan and against Jabin:

> *So God subdued on that day Jabin the king of Canaan before the children of Israel. And the hand of the children of Israel prospered, and prevailed against Jabin the king of Canaan, until they had destroyed Jabin king of Canaan.*
>
> Judges 4:23-24

> **Shake those keys in the face of the enemy and tell him, "Look who has the keys now!"**

When the enemy comes to hold you back and keep you down, depressed and defeated, you need to look at some keys. If nothing else, use your car keys. Shake those keys in the face of the enemy and tell him, "Look who has the keys now!" The most important thing is to shake yourself loose.

Our Lord has said:

"Don't be afraid! I am the First and the Last. I am the living one who died. Look, I am alive forever and ever! And I hold the keys of death and the grave."
Revelation 1:17-18, NLT

That Woman of Battle

Toward the beginning of this chapter, I described a woman of valor, dressed in the armor of God and standing on the battlefield. She was swinging her sword in the heat of the battle and carrying the wounded out to safety, when suddenly the enemy hit her hard, and she fell first to her knees and then to the ground, and her visions and dreams fell there with her on that battleground. I said then that I thought that woman might be you. If that's true, you have heard the taunts of the enemy, that it's too late for you, that your ministry will never revive, that you will never be able to finish your course or successfully run your race. But there is more to what I have seen.

I see the enemy standing back in fear as he begins to hear a new sound in the Spirit. This is not a sound of defeat, but of victory. I see that woman on her knees beginning to sing a song that only angels and the twenty-four elders of Revelation have known. She is singing,

"Holy! Holy! Holy is the Lamb of God!" And she sings it over and over again.

Then, slowly, she begins to get up, and she's looking the enemy right in the face, as she continues to sing boldly: "Holy! Holy! Holy is the Lamb of God!" At that, the enemy turns and runs from that place. Her song has become a great battlecry, and with it, she has defeated the enemy. "Holy! Holy! Holy is the Lamb of God!"

If the Shoe Fits ...

If Deborah's slipper (or even Jael's slipper) fits your foot, allow the sweet Holy Spirit to slip it right now onto your foot. And let a song of overcoming be placed in your heart. Just as Deborah sang over the Lord's victory, the Lord now sings over you.

> *On that day the announcement to Jerusalem will be, "Cheer up, Zion! Don't be afraid! For the* Lord *your God has arrived to live among you. He is a mighty savior. He will rejoice over you with great gladness. With his love, he will calm all your fears. He will exult over you by singing a happy song."*
>
> Zephaniah 3:16-17, NLT

Wow! Just think! Jesus is singing, not only because of you, but He is singing *to* you.

Amen!

Chapter 12

The Bride's Slipper

Then I saw a new heaven and a new earth, for the first heaven and the first earth had passed away, and there was no longer any sea. I saw the Holy City, the new Jerusalem, coming down out of heaven from God, prepared as a bride beautifully dressed for her husband.

Revelation 21:1-2, NIV

Now, little one, we are coming to what some might call the end of your journey, but, after spending this time with you, I don't feel that it's the end of your journey at all. In fact, I feel that you've just begun to step into the fullness of a bright and wonderful season of your life.

You hold the keys to your new beginning. I see the oils of healing flowing all around you, bringing healing to every wound you've had. Where you once stood in defeat, I see you now dancing in the anointing of restoration.

Honey, you will see great battles in this life and in ministry, but you will come through them all. True happiness comes from being in the perfect will of God.

So now, woman of valor, walking in fullness of power and authority, begin to sing "Holy! Holy! Holy!" for the past is gone. Your mind is renewed and you have overcome by the blood of the Lamb and the word of your testimony. Don't look back anymore. Go forward with your life and ministry. The only thing in front of you is a victorious future, starting today.

The Lord has the perfect slipper for you. It was made especially for His Bride, and He has chosen you to wear it. No more will you wear the rags of hopelessness or live in the ashes of your old life. Jesus has just the perfect slipper for you, and His healing virtue is giving you *"beauty for ashes."*

Farewell, for Now

John's Revelation continues with these words:

He will wipe every tear from their eyes. There will be no more death or mourning or crying or pain, for the old order of things has passed away. He who was seated on the throne said, "I am making everything new!" Then he said, "Write this down, for these words are trustworthy and true." Revelation 21:4-5, NIV

And *"these words"* are for you. So, as I say farewell for now, my new friend, smile and enjoy the slipper Jesus has placed upon your life. I want to leave you with these words: When someone asks you, "Are you a Cinderella?" simply reply, "Of course I am. I'm the Bride of the King."

Amen!

Ministry Page

If the Lord has touched you through the pages of this book, changing you or healing you, or if you have asked Him into your heart or rededicated your life to Him as a result of what you've read, I would love to hear from you. E-mail me today and, if you want, send me your testimony and a photo, and I'll put them on our web site or share them in our meetings, so that others can be touched through your restored life. Contact me in any of the following ways:

Dr. Jody Amato
P.O. Box 1596
Walker, LA 70785

www.jodyamatoministries.org
(225) 235-7480
jodyamato@bellsouth.net

— *Notes* —

— *Notes* —

— *Notes* —

Printed in the United States
95298LV00003B/154-249/A

9 781934 769003